# Ethos and Identity

*Three Studies in Ethnicity*

A. L. Epstein

# Ethos and Identity

*Three Studies in Ethnicity*

LONDON
TAVISTOCK PUBLICATIONS
ALDINE PUBLISHING COMPANY
CHICAGO

*First published in 1978*
*by Tavistock Publications Limited*
*11 New Fetter Lane, London EC4P 4EE*

ISBN 0 422 76360 8 (hardback)
ISBN 0 422 76370 5 (paperback)

*and by Aldine Publishing Co.,*
*529 South Wabash Avenue,*
*Chicago, Illinois 60605*

ISBN 0 202 01165 8 (hardback)

*Typeset by Red Lion Setters, Holborn, London.*
*Printed in Great Britain at*
*the University Printing House*
*Cambridge*

© *A.L. Epstein 1978*

This was to have been Scarlett's book.
Instead we agreed
that it should be dedicated
to the memory of
Max Gluckman

# CONTENTS

# PREFACE

'Anyone who ever saw Denis Law play for his country could not
fail to detect the joyful anger in everything he did. Even Bill
Shankly [the former manager of Liverpool Football Club], that
irreplaceable pillar of English football, admits that when he wore
the blue shirt of Scotland the lion on his chest used to roar up at
him: "Get out and get into these English bastards."'

So, a few years ago wrote a sports correspondent of the London
*Observer*, previewing a forthcoming football match between
England and Scotland. If the Scots took on the English at snakes
and ladders, he comments, they would somehow contrive to make
a battle of it. In the world of sport we look for commitment and
partisanship; in the international arena in particular not only have
we become accustomed to powerful expressions of national
fervour, but we also deem such behaviour as proper and legitimate
(provided it is kept within reasonable bounds) and consider it
strange if it is lacking. In recent years, however, we have been
confronted on all sides by numerous instances where similar kinds
of loyalty and allegiance have been mobilized towards social ends
far removed from the realm of sport. In many countries of the
Third World, striving to emerge from a colonial past towards new
independent nationhood, but no less in highly industrialized countries like the United States with its ethnically heterogeneous

population or even the seemingly once-stable United Kingdom, we have become increasingly witness to the struggles of various groups, part of the fabric of a wider social system or polity, to assert their own distinctiveness and claims to autonomy.

The phenomenon has come to be referred to as ethnicity, and many find it puzzling if not actually disturbing. Its widespread incidence, no less than its political significance, accounts in large measure for the interest it has aroused among social scientists; but no less important has been the theoretical challenge that it presents, for ethnicity flies in the face of so much of the conventional sociological wisdom as well as of liberal dogma. As Glazer and Moynihan (1975:7) have recently put it, 'as against class-based forms of social identification and conflict — which of course continue to exist — we have been surprised by the persistence and salience of ethnic-based forms of social identification and conflict'. In a word, ethnic groups have taken on a new lease of life when in theory they were supposed to be disappearing.

Sociologists and social anthropologists have adopted a variety of approaches to the problem. In much of the earlier literature, particularly in the United States, ethnic groups were defined as cultural groups whose behaviour was to be analyzed within a context of assimilation and cultural change. More recent studies have sought to develop alternative models that accorded better with the social realities. Some, for example, have treated ethnic groups as categories of interaction to be examined within a framework of 'situational analysis'. For others ethnicity is essentially a political phenomenon; ethnic groups are interest groups exploiting parts of their traditional culture in order to articulate informal organizational functions that serve in the struggle of these groups for power within the formal political structure. Yet others have stressed the subjective aspects of ethnic affiliation and have gone on to focus on the problems of boundary maintenance. I have gained much from these various approaches, but for reasons discussed in my first essay I find that each of them reveals certain inadequacies. In my own case, interest in the problem was in a sense thrust on me by the circumstances prevailing in the areas where I have carried out my anthropological field research. It would have been impossible to present any analysis of social life on the Copperbelt (of what is now Zambia) in the fifties that did not take full account of 'tribalism'. Later, working among the Tolai of New Guinea, a people who have experienced profound changes in their way of life over the past hundred years, I found myself asking how such groups manage to survive as groups at all, and why they should strive so consciously to retain their sense of group identity. At the same time, I am keenly aware that if I achieved any insight into these situations it was because they touched some chord of response that echoed my own ethnic experience as a Jew of the Diaspora. Reflecting on all this, the one major conviction that emerged was the powerful emotional charge that appears to surround or to underlie so much of ethnic behaviour; and it is this affective dimension of the problem that seems to me lacking in so many recent attempts to tackle it.

The approach I have adopted here seeks to meet this particular difficulty, as well as a number of others, by placing the concept of identity at the heart of the analysis. My first essay, therefore, is devoted to exploring the parameters of the concept through the presentation of a number of ethnographic 'profiles' drawing mainly on my own material from the Copperbelt and the Tolai as well as on the extensive literature available on American Jewry. The aim here, and indeed throughout the volume, is avowedly experimental, for not the least valuable aspects of an approach through identity are in drawing attention to areas where the existing empirical data are inadequate, and in suggesting problems that merit more systematic enquiry.

The concept of identity has of course been much discussed by psychoanalysts, and it will become evident that my own thinking about it has been much influenced by their writings. Since there are some social scientists for whom the introduction of a concept of identity into the discussion of ethnicity appears to smack of 'subjectivism', an unwarranted intrusion of psychology into what is essentially the domain of sociology (see, e.g. Cohen 1974a; Magubane 1969), the matter is perhaps worth dwelling on for a moment.

It should be said at once that if social anthropologists take over from the psychoanalysts a concept such as identity, it does not follow that they will put it to work in the same way or for the same purposes. Indeed, this is most unlikely since their problems are very different. Thus an anthropologist interested in ethnicity is likely to concern himself with questions about the emergence of ethnic groups and categories, the relations between them, and the forces which keep them in being or lead to their decline. By contrast, the concern of the clinician is of course the individual; it lies in the complex process by which the patient's image of self has been achieved, and how it has come to be impaired. So for many psychoanalysts the process is seen essentially as an intra-psychic one; but even in the case of more sociologically-orientated analysts, most notably perhaps Erik Erikson, for whom identity formation always involves the interplay of endogenous and exogenous factors, it is still the individual who provides the point of departure for discussion. Given this divergence of interest, in what way can the concept be helpful, or indeed relevant, to the concerns of the anthropologist? The answer, I believe, lies in the fact that, with its primary emphasis on perception of the self, focussing on identity not only suggests new perspectives on old dilemmas, but also draws attention to aspects of the problem that have hitherto been overlooked.

It is now commonly agreed that it is meaningful to talk of ethnicity only where groups of different ethnic origin have been brought into interaction within some common social context. In one of its aspects, then, ethnicity serves as a system of social classification; it provides a set of categories, with ethnic labels, in terms of which people structure their environment and govern certain of their relations with others. From a sociocentric point of view, these categories are 'objective', external to the individual, compelling him to take cognizance of them; they are collective representations in the full Durkheimian sense. However, by introducing the concept of identity, we are at once reminded that this is only one side of the coin, for every act of identification implies a 'we' as well as a 'they'. From this point of view, ethnicity always has a dual aspect. This has a number of important implications. In the first place, the distinction which follows between the actor's and the observer's perception of a situation, now a commonplace in other anthropological contexts, serves to explain a variety of seeming inconsistencies commonly reported in much ethnic behaviour, as I hope my later analyses will show. Second, it suggests that a view of ethnic groups 'from without', i.e. simply in their external relations and interactions, needs to be supplemented by one 'from within'. While this does postulate a 'subjective' aspect as a counterpart to the 'objective' one, it does not mean that ethnic identity is to be understood or treated in purely endogenous terms.

As with ego identity in Erikson's conception, ethnic identity formation too is a function of the interplay of internal and external variables as these operate within a given social environment. Ethnic identity, no more than ego-identity, is neither given nor innate; the way in which it is generated is always a psychosocial process.

At this point it may be worth stressing that to talk of ethnic identity in a polyethnic context is not to say that it is the only identity, or even the major one, that people may develop or acquire; it is only one among a number of possibilities that may be available to them. This poses crucial problems for analysis. Thus one of the factors which gives the issue its contemporary salience is the way in which ethnicity so often comes to be intricately interwoven with questions of dominance, hierarchy, and social stratification. I take up this problem in my second essay. This essay addresses itself in the first instance to the question of why a reputation for military prowess gained in the pre-colonial past should have any relevance to the according of prestige among the many ethnic groups represented in the African population of the towns of the Copperbelt. Yet it has become apparent that a system of ethnic ranking has developed there in which former military dominance tends to coincide with a position of advantage that certain groups have come to acquire within the occupational structure. What I have sought to bring out here is how certain values from the past are transposed to the towns where they acquire new meaning as people put them to use in structuring their new environment and ordering their social relationships with others. However, this discussion also serves to focus attention on another cardinal facet of identity: the question of continuity. Clearly the problem that confronts the anthropologist studying ethnicity is rather different from that which presents itself to the psychoanalyst; since ethnicity arises so often in circumstances of social upheaval and transformation, which are frequently accompanied by severe cultural erosion and the disappearance of many customs that might serve as marks of distinctiveness, a critical issue is how that identity is to be maintained over a number of generations. This is where history assumes an especial importance in ethnic identity formation, not so much in providing an authentic record of what actually happened in former times, nor in tracing the path of historical development to show how the present has grown out of the past, but rather in providing people with a perception of their past, enabling them through the selective stressing of certain values to make positive identifications with their forebears.

The question of continuity leads in turn to further questions about the way in which the sense of ethnic identity is transmitted. History, of course, can be taught formally, and there are many other ways in which the sense of ethnic identity can be consciously fostered. We know little as yet of how that sense of identity is awakened and grows in the individual, but there seem good grounds for assuming that the process begins early in childhood, and becomes intimately linked with the unconscious identifications that are made with early attachment figures. This is the theme I have sought to explore in my final essay on the role of the grandparents in the formation of ethnic identity. It is in the experience of childhood, I suggest, that the roots of ethnic identity are laid down, acquiring in the process that emotional charge that can make it such a potent force in later life.

We are brought back to the point with which this preface began: the affective dimension of ethnic identity. I have stressed that in a polyethnic situation ethnic identity offers only one among a number of possible forms of social identification. For the individual, therefore, whether, and to what extent, he acquires a sense of ethnic identity always involves some element of choice. But such choice is subject to a number of constraints. Some of these are clearly social, and relate to certain features of the social system; in some societies the opportunities for shedding one's ethnic identity and adopting a class or other social identity may be greater than in others. The more the freedom of choice in this regard, the greater the importance that is assumed by a second set of constraints: the various elements, particularly unconscious ones, that have entered into the building up of one's image of self. Polyethnic situations by their very nature throw people together of diverse origins and backgrounds; such situations are a source of confusion and uncertainty which highlight the vulnerability of the individual and compel new confrontations with the self. Within the circle of one's ethnic associates, however, there is a haven that offers respite and security; among kin and friends there are not only 'shared understandings', there is also trust and appreciation and the opportunity these provide to restore tarnished self-esteem and a sense of one's own worthiness. Such circumstances are likely to favour a strong identification with the ethnic group so that it becomes, as it were, an extension of the self. The health, happiness, and affairs of other members become matters of one's own concern. Conversely, any threat or hint of danger to the group is perceived as though it were a threat to oneself, and may provoke the same angry or even violent response.

In all of these ways, I believe, the concept of identity has much to offer in unravelling the tangled problem of ethnicity. Beyond this, it also seems to me to point in the direction of the wider study of what I may term the social anthropology of affect, where the emotional dimension of human behaviour comes to be given no less weight than the social and intellectual ones.

I have been toying with the ideas that have gone into these essays over a number of years. It was the happy chance of an invitation to spend the academic year 1974-75 as a Fellow at the Center for Advanced Study in the Behavioral Sciences at Palo Alto that alone has enabled me to bring them together in their present form. The idyllic surroundings of the Center, and the unique facilities it offers scholars, have prompted many voices to songs of praise. I am delighted to join the chorus. Nor should I overlook here my debt to the two institutions that made my fieldwork possible: the Rhodes-Livingstone Institute at Lusaka (now the Institute of African Studies, University of Zambia) and the Research School of Pacific Studies at the Australian National University, Canberra.

In the preparation of the essays I have incurred debts to a number of people. Professor Clyde Mitchell, colleague and friend from Copperbelt days, went to a great deal of trouble to provide me with certain quantitative data that I required, though he is not responsible for the uses to which I have put it. At the Center itself, Professor Herman Stein proved to be a mine of information about the Jewish community in the United States, though again the fault is not his if sometimes I have missed the path. I received much encouragement from another fellow Fellow, Professor Aaron Wildavsky, who became interested in what I was doing, read substantial chunks of my manuscript, and came back for more. To all of these I am extremely grateful. Earlier versions of the second essay were delivered at seminars at the School of Oriental and African Studies, University of London, and in the Department of Anthropology, University of Washington, Seattle. I wish to thank

Dr David Parkin and Professor Pierre van den Berghe for making these valuable visits, when I received a number of helpful comments, possible for me.

My original intention was that when completed the volume would carry a dedication to my wife Scarlett. Then while we were still at the Center there came the sad news of the death of Professor Max Gluckman. Max has been an important figure in both our lives, and will always hold a special place in our hearts. Scarlett immediately accepted my suggestion that I should offer these essays in tribute to his memory.

# 1. EXPLORING ETHNIC IDENTITY

'If I am I, simply because I am I, and thou art thou simply
because thou art thou, then I am I and thou art thou. But if I am
I because thou art thou, and thou art thou because I am I, then I
am not I and thou art not thou.'

Rabbi Mendel of Kotzk (cited in Leslie 1971:145)

## Introduction

In their book *The Analysis of Social Change* Godfrey and Monica
Wilson (1954) took their anthropological observations in Central
Africa as the basis for a more general discussion of the nature of
social change. Their point of departure was the view that the
difference between the traditional 'tribal' societies of the region
and the contemporary form of society that had developed there,
between 'primitive' and 'civilized' society, was one of size. In the
former, comparatively few people were in close relationship and
the characteristics of these societies were correlates of their small-
ness of scale. By scale the Wilsons meant the numbers of people
linked by social relationships in space and time, and the intensity of
those relationships. Social change accordingly was a function of an
increase in scale: as scale increased, a complex and interrelated
series of changes took place throughout the entire social system. An
important corollary stemming from this, the Wilsons suggested,
was that intensity in the narrower circles of relations necessarily

diminished as intensity in the wider ones increased; so, for example, the importance of kinship bonds declined and local patriotism was diminished as wider loyalties developed.

Writing more recently, another British social anthropologist, Lucy Mair, has made similar use of the concept of scale in examining developments in the new nations that had emerged in the meantime from their former colonial tutelage; at a number of points she has been able to develop the Wilsons' analysis by making explicit what was often only implicit in their discussion. Mair, for example, takes up the theme of the absorption of rural immigrants into the new towns of Africa, which she compares with the processes of immigration elsewhere. 'As the immigrants find their way about, they begin to merge more and more with the population, provided that no obstacle is put in their way; in an American or western European city the next generation reveal their origin in little but their name.' (Mair 1963:134). The assumption appears to be that in the intermingling of peoples, so characteristic of life in modern towns and cities, ethnic ties and loyalties rapidly disappear. Such an assumption, however, rests on no very substantial bedrock of fact. So far as the American scene is concerned, as we shall see presently, Mair's judgment betrays a lack of caution that can only be attributed to lack of familiarity with the more recent literature on ethnicity there. As to Africa itself, her conclusion is plainly at odds with the assessment of other observers who, like Cohen (1974a:ix), find that 'tribes ... are everywhere becoming integral parts of new state structures and are thus being transformed into ethnic groups with varying degrees of cultural distinctiveness'. Geertz (1963) is clearly referring to the same phenomenon in describing how what he calls the strength of primordial attachments finds its expression in many different places in a wide variety of forms: linguism in India, racialism in Malaysia, or regionalism in Indonesia.

But if what I shall henceforth refer to as the phenomenon of ethnicity poses particularly awkward problems for those countries recently emerged from colonial dependence, it is by no means confined to such areas. And what is interesting to note here is that when we turn to its sociological analysis in a modern industrialized society such as the United States we find that until quite recently many American scholars shared the same assumptions as their colleagues in Africa, even though they worked quite independently of one another and, so it would seem, without much knowledge of one another's writings. The reasons are not difficult to discover. For while anthropologists like the Wilsons or Lucy Mair were chiefly concerned to interpret empirical data drawn from various parts of Africa, they wrote within the framework of a sociological tradition that had become firmly established in western Europe. Of course a number of different strands enter into that tradition. In the work of Godfrey and Monica Wilson the influence of Durkheim is both direct and acknowledged; in the writings of many of the earlier American urban sociologists, such as Louis Wirth, it is the intellectual debt to such figures as Tönnies and Max Weber that is more pronounced. But whatever the particular analytic categories employed, whether, that is to say, their appeal was to the dichotomy of mechanical/organic solidarity, of gemeinschaft/gesellschaft, or to some variant of these, common to all approaches was the premise that modern urban and industrial society, though growing out of earlier forms, was qualitatively different from anything that had gone before. Thus classical sociological analysis proceeded by way of polar opposition: where traditional society stressed family, kinship, and the spirit of community, in modern society such primary bonds gave way to the association as the dominant mode of organization; where interaction in rural society took place between 'whole' persons on a face-to-face basis, in towns social relations were primarily determined by the cash nexus and the labour market, and the contacts of the city tended to be impersonal, superficial, transitory, and segmental (see, e.g. Wirth 1938). Such views had very clear implications for the perception of the problem of ethnicity.

American sociologists were influenced, however, not only by the ideas of the great European theoreticians, but also by their own immediate experience. In certain regards, at least, the problems that confronted the American society of their day were more akin to those of the new nations of Africa and elsewhere than to those of Western Europe, for the onset of urbanization and industrialization in the United States coincided in time with an influx of immigrants on a massive and unprecedented scale from almost every corner of the world. It is interesting in this connection to find Mair, in her account of the new towns of Africa, making use of the metaphor of the melting pot. For the melting pot, in which people of many and diverse backgrounds would be fused into a group sharing a single national culture and identity, provided for a long time a vivid image of American aims and aspirations.

The ideology of the melting pot was acceptable to administrators, politicians, and others concerned with issues of public policy, but it also informed the work of many social scientists. For a time, indeed, according to Berman (1968:47), the behavioural science consensus tended towards the view that social harmony and individual security were best served when minority groups gave up their distinctive characteristics and 'sought full membership in the dominant group'. To advocate such views, indeed, must have appeared as little more than recognition of the empirical realities and the desire to hasten processes already well under way. Thus, in their pioneering study of ethnic communities in Yankee City, carried out in the early thirties, Warner and Srole (1945:155) were moved to observe that the melting pot did not fuse the diverse ethnic elements into a new amalgam; the system worked rather to achieve the transmutation of diverse ethnic elements into elements almost homogeneous with its own. In the light of this assessment we are not wholly surprised, therefore, when we find Warner and Srole winding up their study with a 'timetable' predicting 'the approximate period necessary for the assimilation of each racial and ethnic group', that is the number of generations required for an entire ethnic group to disappear. This period varies for different groups, but the general conclusion to which they are led (1945:295) is that 'the future of American ethnic groups seems to be limited; it is likely that they will be quickly absorbed. When that happens one of the great epochs of American history will have ended ...'

Today, some thirty years on, that day seemingly is still fairly remote. Certainly, American social scientists can still find much in the various dimensions of ethnicity to puzzle over and absorb their attentions. The persistence of ethnic voting provides an example. Thus a paper by Parenti (1967) begins by posing the question why in the face of increasing assimilation ethnic voting persists to about the same degree as in earlier decades, and a little later refers to another study which concludes that 'melting pot or not, ethnic voting may be with us for a long time to come'. Some writers, indeed, go even further and question whether the melting pot idea has any contemporary relevance at all. Glazer and Moynihan (1963:v), for example, comment that the point about the melting pot is that it did not happen: 'the notion that the intense and unprecedented mixture of ethnic and religious groups in American life was soon to blend into a homogeneous end product has outlived its usefulness, and also its credibility.'

My point here, however, is not merely to illustrate the hazards of prediction where human behaviour is concerned. Perhaps it is still too early to claim that Warner and Srole, or the Wilsons and Mair, and others who have shared their assumptions have been shown conclusively to be wrong. What I think can be claimed is that the phenomenon of ethnicity is evidently much more complex than earlier analyses allowed. Consequently we find that more recent discussions of the question reveal important shifts in the general understanding of ethnic groups. Glazer and Moynihan (1974:33), for example, in their latest treatment of the issue, note that where formerly such groups tended to be seen as survivals from an earlier age, and therefore doomed to extinction, there was now a growing sense that they may be forms of social life that are capable of renewing and transforming themselves. I shall discuss some of the more recent approaches to ethnicity later in this essay. For the moment I wish merely to record my view that one of the major weaknesses of earlier analyses was the failure to give adequate weight to the cognitive and affective dimensions of ethnicity. In other words, if we are to understand what Glazer and Moynihan refer to as 'the persisting facts of ethnicity', then I believe that we need to supplement conventional sociological perspectives by paying greater attention to the nature of ethnic identity. Ethnic identity is an expression that recurs frequently in the literature, but there has been little attempt to develop it systematically as a concept of possible heuristic value. The purpose of the present essay is to try and clarify my own understanding of the concept, and so lay the groundwork for exploring ethnic identity in its various facets and dimensions. In pursuing these aims, we shall need to take up such questions as how the sense of collective identity is generated, transmitted, and perpetuated; how new social identities come to be formed and their interaction with pre-existing ones; and the circumstances in which established identities are abandoned or simply disappear.

### Identity: some preliminary soundings

In his novel *Cards of Identity*, Nigel Dennis (1955:118) has one of his characters say: 'Identity is the answer to everything. There is nothing that cannot be seen in terms of identity. We are not going to pretend that there is the slightest argument about *that*.' As the term found its way into the fashionable vocabulary of the day, identity appeared to provide an apt, if nebulous, way of referring to many of the eternal dilemmas of human existence, as is evident in a spate of books that began to appear in the fifties that included the word in their titles. For example, in his book *The Quest for Identity*, Wheelis (1958), although a practising psychoanalyst, avowedly uses the expression not as a technical psychological concept but 'in its ordinary lay meaning'. This turns out, however, as Lichtenstein (1963:186) observes, to be little more than 'a vaguely metaphysical concept, another term for "human nature"', leading to questions that are 'answerable only by a god'.

For present purposes we require a more mundane approach, a more restricted use of the term which will be helpful in handling the particular data we seek to comprehend. Although psychoanalysts disagree among themselves how identity should be defined, their frequent discussions of the question are a measure of their concern to develop it as a rigorous psychological concept. Identity itself finds no place in the classical Freudian terminology.[1] Its increasing use among psychoanalysts appears to have developed as the focus of theoretical interest shifted from the early preoccupation with the id towards the exploration of the ego, a development itself linked to changes in the forms of mental illness that analysts were being called upon to treat. A case described by Gyomroi (1963) serves to illustrate the clinical problem. The patient was a young woman who had spent part of her childhood in a German concentration camp. When first interviewed by the analyst she explained: 'I am not a person, I am always somebody else.' And this, Gyomroi comments, was what formed the core of her pathological behaviour. 'Every day her hair was done differently; she moved in a different manner; it was impossible to see a real person behind the various roles she played.' In more technical language, here was an individual who had lost, more accurately perhaps had never acquired, an ego-identity. What this involves, as Jacobson (1964:23) puts it, is an awareness of the self as a differentiated but organized entity which is separate and distinct from its environment, an entity moreover that has continuity and direction, and the capacity to remain the same in the midst of change.

As the incidence of classical neuroses in the form of hysteria, phobias, and the like declined, psychoanalysts found themselves having to deal increasingly with what came to be known as disorders of character. In these circumstances every patient who enters upon treatment embarks in some sense on a quest for the self; as Reik (1948:173) has remarked, every psychoanalysis that is not superficial leads to the question 'Who am I?' in terms of psychological reality. The concern with identity here is thus individual and psychiatric, and much of psychoanalytic theory, therefore, has developed around questions of identity formation as an intrapsychic process. However, some psychoanalysts, most notably Erik Erikson, have taken a more sociological approach. Erikson too sees the achievement of identity as an ordered and structured psychic process which continues throughout the life of the individual. Where he parts company with his professional colleagues, however, is in refusing to focus simply, or even primarily, on psychic factors; he insists rather on the need to give full weight to somatic and social ones. In the traditional case history, Erikson (1968:44) points out, the patient's residence, ethnic background, and occupation are the first items to be radically altered when it is necessary to disguise his personal identity. The inner dynamics of the case, it is assumed, are thereby left intact. Erikson himself takes a very different view: contemporary social models, he argues, are both clinically and theoretically relevant and cannot be shunted off by brief and patronizing tribute to the role 'also' played by 'social factors'. In a word, as the whole corpus of his writings attests, in dealing with questions of identity formation one is dealing with a process that is 'located in the core of the individual and yet also in the core of his communal culture'.

There is much here that is relevant to my own concerns, and I shall have occasion to return to some of these issues later in this essay. For the moment, at the risk of stating the obvious, it is important to remember that concepts are developed to handle particular problems, and that the nature of these problems is likely to depend in turn on the primary data of observation. Thus, as Bowlby (1961:319) has suggested, we may be led to a different view of the nature of grief and mourning if our primary data are drawn from the observation of actual children as distinct from the reconstruction of infantile experience patiently achieved by plumbing the memory of an adult analysand. In much the same way here, despite Erikson's concern with ego-identity as a psycho-social process, a function of the interdependence of the inner and social organization, it is still the individual who provides him with his point of departure, his basic perspective, whether this be a child struggling to master his own aggressive impulses, a marine, a casualty of war who has lost his inner sense of integrity, or a great historical figure such as Martin Luther or Mahatma Gandhi. In my own case the primary data stem from sociological observation of ethnic behaviour on the Copperbelt of Zambia and in New Guinea, supplemented and informed by my own ethnic experience as a Jew. But if there are differences in our point of entry to the problem, there is at least one regard in which it may be profitable to follow Erikson's advice. The more one writes about identity, he has said, the more the word becomes a term for something unfathomable as it is all-pervasive. 'One can only explore it by establishing its indispensability in various contexts.' (Erikson 1968:9). In what follows I have tried to do precisely this by examining ethnicity in two areas in which I have carried out anthropological field research. In addition, because I consider it important to discuss the issue in other than colonial or post-colonial situations, I have selected for treatment the position of Jews in the United States on which there is now an extensive literature.

### 'Tribalism' on the Copperbelt

From the early days of this century Africans throughout what had recently become Northern Rhodesia, and now the independent nation of Zambia, had been leaving their homes in the villages to seek work and adventure abroad. Some went to the coal-fields of Wankie in what was then Southern Rhodeisa, or travelled even further south to the Union of South Africa; others preferred to remain closer to home and made their way to the zinc and vanadium mines recently opened at Broken Hill (now Kabwe) or crossed the border into the Katanga in the former Belgian Congo (now Zaire). With the development of the Copperbelt in the early thirties what had been a steady trickle of labour migrants quickly became a flood as thousands of Africans from every part of the country, and even beyond, began to converge on the new mine townships of Nkana-Kitwe, Mufulira, and Luanshya or the administrative and commercial centre and rail-head at Ndola. At the time

I carried out my field studies on the Copperbelt in the early fifties, there were about a quarter of a million Africans living in the Copperbelt towns, and the urban population was growing apace from day to day.[2] Meanwhile urban growth was also proceeding rapidly at Broken Hill, Lusaka, now the country's capital, and Livingstone, close by the Victoria Falls.

By their very presence there, Africans had an abiding impact on the character of these towns, giving them some of their most distinctive features (see Epstein 1967). But in the main they came to towns in whose creation they had had no say, and whose central institutions had been developed by the expatriate Europeans for their own purposes. To the extent that they wished to remain in town, therefore, the new African urban-dwellers found themselves compelled to make a variety of adjustments in almost every aspect of behaviour; on the Copperbelt, they quickly discovered, the rhythm of social life was set not by the seasons but was regulated, to borrow Louis Wirth's expressive phrase, 'by the traffic light and the factory whistle'.[3] Moreover, there was little, so it appeared, in their traditional background to help them in this process of accommodation; on the contrary, there was much that was at odds with the new requirements and demands of life in the towns. The migrants came from many different groups; although these might vary considerably in their modes of social organization or in aspects of custom and culture, to be a tribesman implied certain broad similarities of experience. It meant, among other things, being brought up in a small village community whose members were linked by ties of kinship and clanship, and whose interactions were patterned on the basis of a body of assumptions, norms, and mutual expectations generally acknowledged within the group. Sometimes the villages were almost completely autonomous groups or were linked tenuously with other like groups in petty chiefdoms, sometimes they were clearly defined units within a highly centralized polity. In either case a person's social status and roles were articulated within a familiar social and political system. What then can be the relevance of being a tribesman in town where questions about the work that one does, and with whom one does it, or where one lives and the kind of accommodation one enjoys, are determined not by customary reciprocities, but are tied to the new relationship of employer and employee, where in a word the dominant pattern of social life is set by the industrial and civic structures? Yet a major feature of Copperbelt life, which cannot escape the eye of the observer, is the significance that continues to be attached to tribe.[4] The immediate task here is to try and discover its meaning in the urban context.

Clyde Mitchell provided the first important leads into the discussion in his short monograph *The Kalela Dance* (1956). *Kalela* is the name of a popular dance that was regularly performed on Sunday afternoons in the African mine compounds and municipal locations on the Copperbelt at the time of Mitchell's and my own fieldwork.[5] The dance exhibited certain interesting features: a 'tribal' dance in the sense that it was performed by a team of dancers all of whose members save one were Bisa and who, in their opening chant, proclaimed their tribal identity, *Kalela* otherwise displayed no traditional elements in regard to the steps or rhythm of the dance, the songs which provided one of its most characteristic features, or in the dress of the performers. Quite to the contrary, the dancers were smartly turned out in European-style dress, while the songs, which frequently lampooned the behaviour of other tribal groups, provided a pungent and often amusing commentary on contemporary African urban life. In order to explain this seeming paradox Mitchell was led to explore the whole system of urban social relationships in which Africans were now involved, and the place of 'tribalism' within it.

The first major conclusion to which this analysis pointed was that the term 'tribe' did not carry the same meaning in the towns that it did in the rural areas; 'tribalism' in urban and rural contexts related to phenomena of quite different orders. Hence when Africans on the Copperbelt acted as 'tribesmen' this could not be interpreted as a simple carry-over of customary values and attitudes into the urban situation. On the contrary, far from being an expression of conservatism, or even inertia, 'tribalism' was a response to the circumstances of urban life itself. For whereas 'tribe' in the rural areas referred to a group of people united in a single social and political system, and sharing in some measure common customs, doctrines, and values, in town it now referred to a category of interaction within the wider urban system.

In a more recent article, in which he seeks to develop the original analysis, Mitchell (1970) has spelled out more clearly what he means by distinguishing 'tribe' as a structure from 'tribe' as a category. Categorization, he points out, is a common reaction in a situation where social relationships are of necessity transitory and superficial but at the same time multitudinous and extensive. In such circumstances people seek means of reducing the complexity of social relations with which they are confronted. They achieve this by classifying those around them into a restricted number of categories. The process operates through the use of a variety of indicators, ethnic badges, to which individuals respond with the appropriate behaviour. In more concrete terms, an African on the Copperbelt having deemed another to belong to some particular tribal category immediately attributes to that person the characteristics he associates with his stereotype of that tribe.

Making use of social distance tests, Mitchell was able to develop this insight to show how Africans on the Copperbelt were able to reduce the hundred or so ethnic groups represented in the urban population to a mere handful of tribal categories. In this way we are presented with a model of social relations among urban Africans in one of its aspects, a kind of overall 'cognitive map' by reference to which the African in town charts his way through the maze created by the fact that so many of those with whom he is in contact, direct or indirect, are total strangers to him.

What then are the elements that go into the production of such 'cognitive maps'? The remarks of a young labourer from the Mwinilunga District in the far west of the country may serve to illustrate some of the processes at work. We happened to meet one Sunday shortly after he had left the municipal location in Ndola where he had gone to meet a friend and watch the dancing together. However, he had not stayed there very long, he explained, because his friend had not appeared and there were only Bemba dancing *Kalela* that day. Since I knew that *Kalela* was not danced by Bemba, I asked whether they were not really Bena Ngumbo whom he had seen. He replied (in Bemba): 'those of us who come from afar know only the Bemba. In just the same way they call us from the far west Kalwena or "Bakusix-o'-clock" even though we are of many different tribes.'[6] Mitchell (1956:22) makes the point that placing someone in a particular category presupposes some knowledge about the person: his language, dress, eating habits, and so on. Such knowledge is likely to be greater in the case of one's own tribal neighbours than of groups further afield. Hence two principles — geographical propinquity and cultural affinity — serve to fix the relationship of members of one tribe to another in the urban context. In the Zambian case, where cultural differences between ethnic groups are not always clear-cut, the two principles frequently overlap in their operation (cf. Mitchell 1974:7).

The direct connection between ethnic classification and the use of stereotypes is evident from Mitchell's account, and the remarks of the young labourer from Mwinilunga also illustrate how on occasion such stereotypes may even be contained within the terms of designation commonly used for particular groups. The stereotype at best is based on partial knowledge only; it is built up around some aspect of behaviour, real or imaginary, which is deemed to be characteristic of the group in question, and which becomes the basis for the evaluation of individuals belonging to that group as well as of the group as a whole. Thus while the system of classification makes frequent use of standard tribal names (e.g. Bemba, Lozi, Lamba, etc.) or other designations which have a clear extra-urban reference, the stereotypes that develop and reinforce that system grow predominantly out of the fragmentary knowledge acquired in the towns themselves. This is seen very clearly in the fact that so many of the stereotypes have a sexual basis. A good deal of casual social interaction among urban Africans of different ethnic origins takes the form of transitory sexual liaisons, and there is much interest in, and exchange of views about, matters pertaining to sex among the different groups. Once, for example, one of my research assistants was paying a personal visit at the home of an older man from the same part of the country as himself. When he reached the house he found his host sitting outside chatting to his next-door neighbour. 'Welcome', called the older man, 'greet my friend here Albert — he's a Kasai from the Congo.'[7] My assistant, a Lunda from the area of Chief Kazembe, had himself spent some time in the Congo, and he and Albert began to converse together in Swahili. Linked thus, their host now broke in and asked them to explain why it was that the Kasai practised male circumcision. Albert replied that Kasai women objected to marriage with 'you Lamba' because men who were uncircumcised ejaculated quickly when they had sexual intercourse, and therefore failed to give their partners full satisfaction. As he proceeded to elaborate on the point in some detail, the older Lunda became rather agitated and at length interrupted: 'Do not shame us with such talk, you heathen, when you know that we "play" regularly with your women.' This was a reference to the fact that all Kasai women on the Copperbelt are regarded by local Africans as prostitutes, a point which Albert was quick to pick up and turn to his own advantage. 'No', he said, 'they sleep with you for francs [i.e. for money]. For that reason they cannot be angry if you do not satisfy them. In fact, the quicker you are the better for that gives them the chance to look for other men.'

The stereotypes of other groups also reveal a strong sexual component. The predilection of the Lamba for adultery is lampooned in one of the stanzas sung by the dancers of *Kalela* (Mitchell 1956:8); similarly, in the *Mbeni* dance of the Bemba, one of the verses acclaims the beauty of the Nsenga women, and concludes with the words *kwela pa lulu umfwe uluweme*, climb on an anthill and you will feel something good. This refers to a position said to be favoured by Nsenga women in the act of intercourse, but their sexual attractiveness is also held to lie in the many rows of beads they wear around the waist as well as in the scarifications which they are prepared to expose to the gaze of a lover. By contrast, Bemba women wear a much smaller number of beads and are commonly thought of as prudish and even frigid; they are said to be unable to 'dance' and some complain that sleeping with a Bemba woman is like 'sleeping with a stone'.

As Mitchell has observed, the situation in which the *Kalela*, *Mbeni*, or similar dances take place has something of the character of a joking relationship, and such attitudes can be expressed without giving offence. But the stereotypes also operate outside the dance arena and, in so far as they enter into actual behaviour, can have more serious consequences. At one time, for example, there was considerable strife at Nkana mine (Kitwe) where Nyakyusa workers (from Tanzania) were aggrieved by the lack of respect accorded them by the Bemba. In particular they complained that Bemba men refused their womenfolk, while Bemba women spurned their men. Bemba themselves told me that they regarded Nyakyusa as an unclean people marked out by certain genital peculiarities. For a Bemba to have intercourse with a Kyusa was therefore regarded as an act of defilement. The holding of such stereotypes makes it clear then that if 'tribalism' is to be seen in the first instance as a system of classification, one also has to recognize that more than purely cognitive processes are at work; the categories are not simply 'neutral' pigeon-holes, they are highly charged with affect.

In his initial discussion in *The Kalela Dance* Mitchell takes what I may term a sociocentric approach to 'tribalism'; it is a global view seen as it were from the outside. He himself has acknowleged this in a recent paper where he notes that the structure of perceptions of social distance among ethnic categories is a general representation which emerges when one combines the somewhat different perceptions characteristic of different sets of respondents (Mitchell 1974:8). The main thrust of the analysis is thus on the interaction *between* categories. So, for example, while he reports that the *Kalela* team which he observed was formed by breaking away from an existing Bisa team, he does not pursue the point further, but emphasizes instead how groups ignore their internal differences in the face of the multi-tribal situation of the towns.[8] In his more recent analyses, however, he appears to have shifted his ground somewhat, referring to the need to distinguish the actor's model from that of the analyst, and to recognize different levels of integration in the process of categorization (Mitchell 1970; 1974).

It seems to me that a much simpler formulation is to recognize that the delineation of social categories is always a two-way process. In differentiating others, that is to say, one is also defining oneself. Hence, ethnic categories always have a dual aspect: they are at one and the same time both 'objective', that is external to, or independent of, the actor, and 'subjective', that is internal to the actor, a perception of the self. To this perception, moreover, both conscious and unconscious mental processes contribute. For just as certain behavioural traits, for example, gestures or a particular gait, which serve to mark one's individuality, are often rooted in infantile identifications, so the sense of self may also be shaped in ways of which one is not consciously aware. From this perspective then, the sense of ethnic identity appears as a function of the interplay of external and internal perceptions and responses, and as the analysis proceeds I hope to clarify it and work out some of the implications that stem from it. For the moment, however, I wish merely to illustrate the general point by referring once more to the question of stereotypes. As I have already observed, stereotypes serve to reinforce one's perceptions of others, but by their very nature they also imply a definition of oneself; they always carry, at least implicitly, a two-way evaluation. Thus, for the Congolese Albert introduced earlier, the practice of male circumcision meant that Kasai men were able to satisfy their wives sexually, whereas others were fit to approach them only as prostitutes. While Lunda might react to this as a public slur on their virility, among themselves they regard circumcision with abhorrence, speaking of a man who is circumcised as *cituto*, a term that in other contexts refers to something that has become blunted, worn out, and useless. In other words, as between different ethnic groups, the practice or non-practice of a custom such as male circumcision has to be regarded as more than a simple diacritical index: viewed from the outside, it may be evaluated negatively and so provide the basis for a stereotype;[9] looked at from the inside, however, it may be evaluated positively and thus acquire new significance as a symbol of identity, that which serves to define 'us'. Its effectiveness as a symbol is also likely to depend on the strength it draws from the meanings that attach to it in the unconscious.

Viewed then in one of its aspects 'tribalism' operates to provide people with a set of categories which enables them to define the situations in which they find themselves and so adopt the modes of behaviour appropriate to them. 'Tribalism' from this point of view might be thought of as a kind of signalling device. Viewed in its aspect as an expression of identity 'tribalism' can also be expected to have a bearing on behaviour in a wide range of contexts. One such area which has received some discussion relates to the emergence of the category known on the Copperbelt as 'home-boys' (Mitchell 1970; 1974). The term itself, which translates the Bemba expression *Bakumwesu*, literally those from our [place], immediately indicates that the category can only have meaning as an act of self-definition.[10] 'Home-boy' ties assume importance in the context of housing and accommodation, particularly for young unmarried migrants, as well as in the building up of personal networks (Epstein 1961a). The role of this category in urban political organization has also been well-documented by Harries-Jones (1969) in his study of Luanshya subsequent to my own. Yet another area, the subject-matter of a preliminary paper by Mitchell (1957), which merits more detailed study, concerns choice of marriage partners and the factors which influence it. Here, however, I want to focus on a topic that has received very little attention in the literature on the Copperbelt: the emergence and functions of tribal associations. In this context we shall see 'tribalism' serving as a principle of organization in social behaviour, and can begin to examine it in its interaction with other principles of organization. Starting, that is to say, with a view from 'within' we can proceed to look at the way 'tribalism' enters into behaviour in an ever-widening field of social relationships.

## Tribal associations

The development of tribal associations has been widely reported as a feature of modern urban life in many parts of Africa. Careful scrutiny of the data, however, shows that these associations are of many different kinds, often cater for different social categories, and serve different ends. Perhaps the kind of association that occurs most frequently is the burial or mutual aid society. Not surprisingly, therefore, tribal associations are often referred to in the literature as having an adaptive role, easing the adjustment of the migrants to the strange surroundings of the town (see, e.g. Little 1965). Whether this is an adequate view or not, it is a curious fact that tribal associations of the common type have not developed on the Copperbelt to anything like the same extent as elsewhere. There are good reasons, therefore, for considering some of the associations which have come into being.

The group on which I was able to gather the most extensive information was the Bemba Tribal Association. This was founded early in 1952 on the initiative of a few young men employed as junior clerks in Government offices at Ndola. Their general aim, as set out in the formal constitution,[11] was to encourage greater understanding and co-operation among Bemba in Ndola such as (the document claimed) they displayed at home. The immediate precipitating factor, however, seems to have been some dissatisfaction with the way the Bemba Tribal Elders were conducting themselves.[12] In one case, for example, the young men had met a Bemba woman at the bus station shortly after her arrival in Ndola where she had come to join her husband. When, having made some enquiries, it was learned that the man had just been transferred elsewhere, they decided to take her to the house of the Bemba Elder who took the name of the chief Mporokoso. When he discovered that she came from another part of Bemba country and was an ordinary commoner (*mupabi*) into the bargain, he apologized and said he was unable to help her.

It was following this and other similar incidents that the young men conceived the idea of forming the Association. Aware that they were too junior to undertake the task on their own, their first step was to consult a number of more senior Bemba, *bakalamba*, who were already well-known and respected within the town. After further discussion it was agreed that the matter should be put to a public meeting. According to my informants, it was quite a large gathering, attended by about 200 people. A point of immediate interest is that the proposal to found the Association met with opposition from some speakers on the grounds that it appeared to separate the Bemba people from the other tribes. However these objections were overborne when the sponsors explained that the Association was not to be a political body, and would concern itself only with internal domestic matters. It was then proposed from the floor that the Bemba member of the African Urban Court, seen in this context as a representative of the Paramount Chief Chitimu-kulu, should be invited to attend and address them at another meeting when the Association would be formally inaugurated and office-bearers elected. The man chosen as President was a carpen-ter and labour-*capitao* or 'boss-boy' working for a firm of Euro-pean contractors, and well-known as an African trade union leader. The Vice-President was also a carpenter; his son, a white-collar worker, and one of the young men on whose initiative the Association was started, was elected Secretary. One of his friends became Vice-Treasurer.

For a time the Association was quite active and regular meetings were called each month. One of the first steps taken was to advise the Location Superintendent of the group's formation. Although there was no legal requirement for the registration of such associa-tions as was the case, for example, in the neighbouring Congo, this was important for gaining official recognition and support. One result was that shortly afterwards the Association arranged elec-tions for new Tribal Elders and was able to win recognition for two additional Bemba representatives.[13] The President himself was nominated, but declined because of his other commitments. The Vice-President and Treasurer received the next highest number of votes and became the new Tribal Elders. As noted, the first of these was father of the Secretary, and took the name of the Bemba chief Nkolemfumu, to whom he was in fact closely related; the other took the name of Mwamba, the title next senior to Chitimukulu in the contemporary hierarchy of Bemba chiefs. Among its other activities was to arrange for a member of the group to attend regularly at the mortuary and to report back the death of any Bemba; the Association then helped in organizing the funeral or in providing for the widow and her children to return to their village. A number of Bemba chiefs, including the Paramount Chief Chitimukulu, visited Ndola during the first year of the Association's life, and they were received and entertained by the Association, which also organized the *chililo* or mourning rites when news was received of the death of Chief Muceleka. However, the records of the Association also show that after a short time interest in its activities began to slacken; when two of the young men who had played the main part in its formation left Ndola towards the end of the year it finally collapsed and was not revived.

Before taking up a number of more general points, it may be helpful to refer briefly to two other groups: the Barotse National Society and the North-western Province Development Association. The first of these was a much larger-scale organization, a product of the widespread Lozi diaspora, claiming to have branches in the Union of South Africa, in Bechuanaland (now Botswana), and in the Rhodesias. At the time of my fieldwork the General Secretary of the Society was at Kitwe on the Copperbelt; there was a branch at Ndola. Moves to form the North-western Province Development Association only began towards the end of 1956 when I was winding up my study. Moreover, although Africans from Ndola took part in the preliminary discussions to form the Association, the meetings were held elsewhere on the Copperbelt and I had no opportunity to attend them. Although, therefore, my information on the three bodies is very uneven, sufficient data is available to point up some of their common as well as contrasting features.

All three groups came into being on the initiative of people who were living in towns and addressed themselves to the problems of those who were far away from their homes in the countryside; all were an expression of a sense of ethnic identity and can be seen as serving to maintain and foster that identity. At the same time there were a number of important differences in aims and purposes as between the groups, pointing to different motives in their formation. The Bemba Tribal Association sought to win legitimacy for itself by writing to the Paramount Chief to inform him of the group's existence, and it maintained relations with other chiefs in Bembaland by writing to them from time to time. Within Ndola it addressed itself to all Bemba and on occasion claimed to act on their behalf. On the other hand, the people who were most actively engaged in its affairs were drawn from only a few areas of Bemba country; the fact that the Association sought the election of additional Tribal Elders rather than the replacement of those already serving in this capacity shows that they were concerned with the proper representation in Ndola of their own provinces within Bembaland. In other respects, however, the Association appears as a very urban-oriented group, the creation of a number of young men anxious to win a place for themselves within the prestige system that had developed within the towns, a point to which I shall return shortly. By contrast, while the Barotse National Society too claimed to speak for all Lozi in the town, its most prominent members gave a good deal of their energies and attention to the internal politics of Barotseland. To a considerable extent, indeed, the Society operated as a political pressure-group, one of whose chief purposes was to gain a voice within the inner councils of Barotse government, so paving the way for the radical reform of the Barotse social and political system, which the Society regarded as being out of keeping with modern democratic ideals and requirements. Finally, in the case of the North-western Province Development Association, the orientation was entirely and explicitly rural. Although the prime movers in its formation appear to have been Western Lunda scattered throughout the towns of the Copperbelt, the aims of the Association (as set out in the constitution) were to create 'an organized, harmonious and advanced community' in the Province, and to seek every means for its economic and political development. Lunda in Ndola explained the underlying motivation: other tribal areas had secondary schools, not their own; many Africans from Northern Rhodesia had now gone for higher education overseas, but none from their own home area; while in the towns, in all the Urban Advisory Councils on the Copperbelt, there were only two members who came from the north-west. Behind the formation of the Association there lay, then, the hope of exerting pressure on the Administration and raising their status as against other areas and groups in both town and country.

A second point of contrast concerns the social categories represented by the leadership of the Associations. We have seen that the Bemba Tribal Association was founded on the initiative of a few junior white-collar workers, while the major titles of honour went to older men who were employed as artisans or labour overseers. One leading official of the African National Congress in Ndola, well-known for his opposition to any manifestation of 'tribalism', joined the Committee later on, but this may well have been with the intention of keeping an eye on the group and ensuring its co-operation with Congress.[14] Other prominent Bemba of the local African 'establishment' refused to be involved. I discussed the matter once with one of these, a man whom I shall refer to as Mulenga, a well-known public figure in a variety of African representative bodies and other organizations. He told me that he had been approached to lend his support to the Association by an African Welfare Officer, also Bemba, but he had declined; had it been an Association open to people of all tribes, he said, he would have been happy to join, but he was opposed to all forms of 'discrimination'. Moreover, he had then persuaded the Welfare Officer himself to withdraw. By contrast, it was precisely members of this social category who dominated the Barotse National Society. One of its leading members on the Copperbelt was President of the African Mines Salaried Staff Association, and the former first President of the Northern Rhodesia Congress, later to be re-constituted as the Northern Rhodesia African National Congress. In the case of the North-western Province Development Association, the two men from Ndola who attended as delegates the preliminary discussions which led to the forming of the group were the Lunda member of the African Urban Court, known in town by the name of the Senior Lunda Chief Shinde, and another man whom I shall call Mkamba. Mkamba was immediately recognizable as a member of the new African urban elite; employed by a firm of lawyers, he was among the most highly paid Africans in Ndola at that time. He was also very active in public life and, like his friend Mulenga, served on many African representative councils and other bodies.

I have mentioned that the emergence of 'tribal societies' has been frequently reported as an important feature of urban life in many parts of contemporary Africa, and in some places at least they appear to have developed quite rapidly as an integral part of the urban social structure. Given the fact that on the Copperbelt 'tribalism' appears as a primary category of interaction, that is, the first significant characteristic to which Africans react to one another, one might well have expected the same development there.

Why this did not occur to anything like the same extent as elsewhere is not only puzzling in itself, but should carry some important clues as to the nature of 'tribalism' there. The institution of a system of Tribal Elders on the Copperbelt at an early date may well be an important factor here. As Mitchell (1956:20) has suggested, the Elders always served as a focus of tribal sentiment. Moreover, recognized and aided by the compound and location authorities, the Elders were often in a position to assume the responsibilities which elsewhere brought tribal associations into being: offering help to new arrivals, organizing gatherings for visiting chiefs, or arranging the funeral of a tribesman who had died in town.[15] Harries-Jones has carried the argument a stage further: showing how the Elders served as nodal points in 'home-boy' networks, he suggests (1969:339) that 'home-boy' ties were both too dispersed and transitory to maintain more permanent forms of association. The material I have presented here allows us to introduce some further considerations, and at the same time raise other questions.

The rise and fall of the Bemba Tribal Association is of particular interest in this connection. Although addressed to all Bemba, the Association did appear to make a special appeal to those with more limited 'home-boy' links. On the other hand, the lead in forming the group was taken by younger, more educated but still little-known town-dwellers for whom, I have suggested, the Association offered an avenue for acquiring prestige and a rung on the ladder of urban leadership. In this regard they had discovered for themselves a path that experience elsewhere has shown can be quite successful, as may be seen for example in Banton's (1957) account of the young schoolmaster in Freetown, Sierra Leone who used the Temne *compins* to revive the flagging sense of Temne identity and at the same time came to provide himself with a very effective power base. The young Bemba clerks were evidently much less successful, but the interesting question is not so much why they failed, but why the solution they adopted had not been tried more frequently. At least part of the answer, I believe, lies in a suggestion made elsewhere (Epstein 1967:281) that tribal associations have to be understood in their relationship to associations of other kinds and to the overall status system of the community. It is not necessary for present purposes to discuss this matter in detail, and I note only a few more general points.

Although tribal societies have been of only marginal significance on the Copperbelt, the area has been very rich in other forms of associational life. For reasons examined at length in an earlier study (Epstein 1958), the first African urban associations to emerge were the Welfare Societies. These drew their membership from the still tiny but rising class of more educated, English-speaking Africans who came together to discuss the social and political problems of the day. These societies amalgamated to form a federation which eventually became the Northern Rhodesia Congress. Some time later when this body was reconstituted as the African National Congress, branches were established in all of the towns, offering opportunities for young people to emerge as branch officials and to win recognition as local personalities. At about the same time there began to come into being a range of other bodies: trade unions and other occupational associations as well as the various official groups representing African interests such as the Urban Advisory Councils and African Housing Boards. All of these bodies operated in the field of Black-White relations, and all demanded an emphasis on African solidarity in opposition to the dominant Europeans. What is more, all the leading positions in these organizations had come to be occupied by members of the new African urban elite, to many of whom 'tribalism' appeared as a thing of the past and an obstacle to their own advancement within a modern society. In such circumstances there was little incentive towards the development of tribal associations when there were so many openings, offering the promise of wider recognition among the populace at large, in the 'pan-tribal' organizations; nor, as we have seen in the case of the Bemba Tribal Association, was the attempt to seek prestige in this way likely to win support among the urban elite whose recognition the sponsors were most anxious to gain.

In considering the case of the Bemba Tribal Association we see that it served as a means of organizing a particular category of people for certain purposes. From this point of view the group served as an expression of the Bemba sense of tribal identity. At the same time it would be quite wrong to see in the formation of the Association the simple persistence of traditional tribal loyalties and allegiances into the urban milieu. On the contrary, its growth and rapid demise have also to be viewed in relation to other principles or organizations at work, in particular the emerging class structure of the towns. In this particular instance, to judge from the comments of one Bemba cited earlier, 'tribe' and 'class' appear as mutually opposed categories, and ethnic identity seems to yield before a newly acquired class identity. That the matter is much more complex than this, however, is made immediately plain in the case of the Barotse National Society or that of the North-western Province Development Association. Important questions then are raised about the nature of the relationship between the categories of 'tribe' and 'class' and its bearing on the images of self developed by Africans in town.

## 'Tribe', 'class', and 'situation'

In seeking a point of entry to the discussion of these issues it will be helpful to return for a moment to the two men whom I introduced earlier: Mulenga and Mkamba. The first, it will be recalled, declined the invitation to join the Bemba Tribal Association as a founding member and persuaded at least one other Bemba to do likewise. Mkamba, by contrast, reacted with enthusiasm to the proposal to set up the North-western Province Development Association and actively participated in the venture. Why should these two men, alike in so many respects and sharing many common ideas and values, have responded so differently to what would seem a basically similar situation? Of course the two men may have been motivated by personal considerations of which I have no knowledge. Even so, I believe that their very different responses also reveal the presence of social factors influencing the perception of 'tribe' among different members of the 'middle class'.

Both Mulenga and Mkamba had spent most of their lives in town, and both men were fully committed to an urban way of life; unless and until circumstances compelled it, neither was prepared to contemplate a return to the rural areas. At the same time both maintained many extra-urban links. Frequently, indeed, they would complain to me about the number of visitors from home they had to entertain or point to the many dependants they maintained. Once I was led to tax Mkamba on the matter and asked him rather bluntly why he continued to accept the burden. He replied simply: 'I'm surprised at you. I thought you knew us Africans better than that.' Mkamba discharged these onerous obligations to his kin and others because it seemed to him unthinkable to do otherwise; at the same time, as we have seen, he also acknowledged in his public behaviour that he was a Lunda. Mulenga too continued to discharge his no less onerous responsibilities, but his status as a Bemba was much more ambiguous and difficult to define. He had grown up away from home, he once explained to me, and there were many respects of customary behaviour with which he was unfamiliar. 'I am a detribalized native', he said, 'and many of the old customs I find quite meaningless.' Yet there was also a pride in being Bemba, a pride he confessed to experience when, for example, working through the membership of the many different organizations on the Copperbelt, he discovered how many of the leading figures in them were Bemba. Against this, he felt very strongly that 'tribalism' separated Africans from one another, and so hindered their general advancement: hence his opposition to the formation of the Bemba Tribal Association.

Much of what I have just recorded emerged in the course of a long conversation lasting some hours and covering many topics. What was very interesting was that as soon as Mulenga turned from talking about himself and his ideas to gossip about local events and personalities he could not prevent himself from resorting to the common stereotypes held by Bemba in regard to other ethnic groups. It was evident, moreover, that Mulenga had not always been successful in persuading others to accept his own image of self. One day, for example, I happened to meet a Lozi of my acquaintance as he was coming out of the office where Mulenga was employed as senior clerk. The Lozi was rather agitated because some forms which he had handed in earlier to the office had been mislaid — in his view, deliberately. 'That man', he said, referring to Mulenga, 'hates all Lozi.'

A matter that once came before a meeting of the African Housing Board in Ndola, of which both Mulenga and Mkamba were members, helps to shed further light on the attitudes and position of the two men and serves at the same time to illustrate some of the complexities that characterize the relationship of 'tribe' and 'class'. The item in question related to the way jobs at the Beer Hall had come to be monopolized by members of a small tribal group, the Inamwanga. This was greatly to be deplored, the speaker who introduced the motion explained, because it led to inefficiency; the Manager could not supervise things properly because if one of the workers did anything wrong his fellows would not be prepared to report him. 'These people are making a tribal thing, they are making a home for themselves so that others cannot be employed there.' The speaker, a former school-master, and now running his own business, was also one of the most influential Tribal Elders in Ndola. What is more, only a short time before I had been present when one of his friends, also on the Board, was reproaching him for not supporting the setting up of a new National Burial Society. 'We have to get away from these tribal jealousies', his friend explained when the other declined on the grounds that his own tribe already had their own burial society.

The first speaker found many supporters. One, a Bemba employed as a clerk in a Government office, recalled how some time before the Namwanga 'boss-boy' had brought about the dismissal of an Ushi employee on a trumped up charge in order to replace him with a fellow Namwanga. Addressing the chairman (the District Commissioner) he commented: 'You may find this strange as a European, but it is the mentality of the African to associate as a tribe.' Mulenga himself said little on this occasion, but indicated support for the motion, as one might have anticipated. Mkamba, however, spoke strongly against taking any action in the matter. Intimating that his friends were not so liberated from 'tribal thinking' as they liked to profess, he reproved them saying 'it is disgraceful that people like ourselves should take up this matter of "tribalism"'. All that mattered was that there were people to do the job properly. He then added somewhat acidly, but very revealingly, 'I have heard no complaint that all of those engaged in the work of night-soil removal happen to be Lovale'. Mkamba's only supporter was a highly respected Tribal Elder, but his command of English was so poor that I could not understand what he was saying.

To the casual observer Mkamba's reference to the Lovale might have appeared simply as a sound debating point, but it was a point made with feeling, reflecting the perspective of a man from the north-west whose peoples, as we have seen, are lumped together as 'Bakusix-o'-clock'. It is apparent then that 'tribe', viewed in its internal aspect, can have a very different meaning for persons of different ethnic groups, even when they are also closely identified with the new 'middle class'. Such perceptions in turn reflect the different positions that the various groups have come to acquire in the urban and national social systems, and the prestige that is attached to each. This is a complex issue, which will recur in other contexts, and which I will also take up again in my second essay. Here, therefore, I focus on another aspect of the problem thrown up by our material: the manifest difficulties that Africans have in dealing with the question of 'tribalism' and the many inconsistencies it appears to generate in their behaviour.

Encountering similar phenomena in my earlier study at Luanshya, I sought to explain Africans' handling of these contradictions by reference to the principle of 'situational selection'. By this I meant to show, for example, how forms of 'tribal' leadership might continue to operate in towns within the field of domestic and interpersonal relations, but that in the political sphere, where quite different sets of interests were involved, such leaders were caught up in a conflict of roles and were replaced by spokesmen with quite different qualifications and of a quite different social stamp (Epstein 1958:227-40). Mitchell has explained the relations of 'tribe' and 'class' in similar 'situational' terms: hence, within a tribal association internal divisions might be expected to find expression in 'class' terms, and within a teachers' or clerks' association in terms of 'tribe'. The emergence of a 'class' category does not automatically lead to the disappearance of 'tribe'; both categories may continue to operate simultaneously, individuals switching from one to the other depending on the nature of the social situation. This view of urban 'tribalism' has been challenged by Mayer. Mayer (1962:580) complains that what he calls the adoption of an 'alternation model' tends towards a schizoid picture of the migrant's social personality. The use of the term schizoid here can only be pejorative, for the argument itself can hardly be taken seriously. What I have called 'situational selection' is only the social expression of a familiar psychological mechanism by which discrepant ideas are segregated in different compartments of the mind; far from engendering schizoid tendencies, it is a device which operates to avoid conflict and without which few of us would be able to get along. A more pertinent criticism that Mayer makes is that such an approach does not help us to understand the 'process of urbanization' among migrants, what he calls a shift in the balance between within-town ties and extra-town ties. To understand how this shift comes about, he argues, it is not enough to concentrate on within-town ties alone. Since men who are employed in towns still discharge 'tribal' roles *pari passu*, the study of migrancy requires that we take account equally of the urban industrial and rural 'tribal' systems.

That there are many features of Copperbelt 'tribalism' that cannot be adequately understood simply by reference to the urban social system is a position that I am not only prepared to accept, but one moreover that I adopted explicitly in my own earlier analysis (1958:237-38). What is important here, however, is how these urban-rural relations are conceptualized. For Mayer a population becomes fully urbanized when the town-dwellers are no longer subject to the pull of the hinterland. At this point it has become a purely urban proletariat (and/or bourgeoisie), and 'tribalism' simply disappears. This formulation suffers a degree of circularity: as long as people retain some sense of ethnic identity they are not fully urbanized; in this way it tends to obscure the very problem that has to be explained — that when one looks at ethnicity in comparative perspective it is frequently found to retain its significance long after people have ceased to be migrants. A more profitable approach, that avoids this particular difficulty, is to recognize that in dealing with ethnicity we are concerned with varying expressions of ethnic identity. In its most elementary aspect identity is a matter of perception, but that perception is shaped and coloured by its social environment. Thus we have seen how circumstances on the Copperbelt encouraged the emergence of 'tribal' categories as entities distinct from the 'tribal' systems of the rural areas. At the same time, it was the rural background of the urban-dwellers, with its associated cultural and ethnic diversity, which provided the basis for the urban system of tribal categories. There are many ways in which that background can remain significant for people in towns, entering into and influencing their view of themselves and others there. In so far as urban Africans continue to play 'tribal' roles, as Mayer suggests, the relations of urban Africans to their tribal chiefs would appear to a topic meriting some attention. Chiefs are the representatives of their tribes, and in presenting some of the material I collected at Ndola on the occasion of visits there by a number of chiefs I hope to carry further the analysis of the meaning that attaches to 'tribe'.

*Urban-dwellers and tribal chiefs*

In 1935 there occurred the first major strike of Africans on the

Copperbelt. Shortly afterwards the Government arranged for a visit there of the Senior Bemba Chief Mwamba, his 'son' Chief Munkonge, and a number of Bemba hereditary Councillors so that they might learn something of the nature of their people's grievances, and at the same time express condemnation of a set of events which 'had brought the name of their tribe into disrepute'. Munkonge was then called as a witness before the Commission of Enquiry set up to enquire into the disturbances. He said: 'I think that we chiefs lose power over these people because they are not under our direct jurisdiction; they are under Europeans here, and we cannot control them ourselves.' Though this was a state of affairs which Munkonge plainly deplored, his statement nevertheless was a simple and accurate assessment of the same social realities that Gluckman (1945) had in mind when he remarked that 'in a sense every African is detribalized as soon as he leaves his tribal area'. In the towns of the Copperbelt, Africans at once come under the jurisdiction of many different authorities, and if chiefs have any sanctions at their disposal they are at best indirect and peripheral. On the other hand, it does not follow that because they lack effective power they are therefore bereft of all significance. In what does that significance consist?

In the first place it becomes clear that for a townsman to be able to claim close kinship with a chief may be not only a source of personal satisfaction, but also a fact which is felt to merit public recognition. Once, for example, an employee of the Welfare Department had been reprimanded by the European officer-in-charge. Later he reported the incident to the senior African in the office, complaining that the European just treated him like dirt; he did not know that he was a son of Chief Mushili. Such episodes were not unusual. I was told of one young trade union official who, when he could not gain his point at a meeting, would give vent to his annoyance by announcing that he was the grandson of Chief Chakumbila, and if he left the Union he could always become a Councillor at home (see also p.124 below).

The behaviour reported in these two instances only makes sense on the assumption that the individuals concerned expected their status as relatives of a chief to be recognized by others. And it is plain from other contexts that such expectations were indeed often met. As we have seen, Tribal Elders took the names of their own chiefs, and almost all claimed to be close kinsmen. The Elders at

Ndola still appeared to enjoy considerable respect among the populace and were addressed as chiefs; when one enquired how a particular Elder had been selected a common reply was 'I don't know, it must be because he is a relative of the chief'. The importance of chieftainship was also seen in the African Urban Court. The five members of the Court at Ndola, nominees of rural Native Authorities whose people were heavily represented in the population of the town, were also referred to as chiefs (*bashamfumu*), and were usually treated with deference as they moved around the town. As mentioned earlier, for the inaugural meeting of the Bemba Tribal Association the Bemba member of the Court was specially invited along to give the opening address. Similarly, the Lunda Court member was a delegate to the meeting called elsewhere on the Copperbelt to launch the North-western Province Development Association. The obverse side of the coin was seen one day in the huge crowd that gathered at the Court to hear a charge of adultery brought against one of the members of the Court itself. There was widespread interest in observing how 'the chiefs would deal with their fellow chief'.

In such ways chieftainship still appears to have a lively interest for Copperbelt Africans. But how widespread or intense is that interest within the general populace? Does it vary as between different social categories or with the length of time spent in town? While working at Luanshya I was led to devise some crude tests of social ranking that might help to shed some light on these questions. Later, Mitchell and I (1962) refined the techniques and carried out a more elaborate experiment using as respondents students at a number of schools and colleges around Lusaka. What emerged from this study was the universally high rating that was accorded the office of chief, even by respondents from groups in which traditionally the institution of chieftainship was not highly developed or was even non-existent. Nevertheless, for a variety of reasons, some of which are touched on below, it is difficult to know what weight to attach to such findings or to infer how they might relate to actual behaviour.

I pursued these questions further at Ndola. There it quickly became evident that at least among members of the elite the question of chieftainship was intimately bound up with the issue of 'tribalism', and generated the same kinds of ambiguity. The matter was once mooted at a meeting of the African Debating Society which was asked to consider the motion that 'in the opinion of this House the institution of chieftainship has no meaning for urban Africans'. Among those who spoke for the motion the most charitable view was that in the towns the chief's traditional functions had been taken over by other specialists — magistrates, ministers of religion, welfare officers, trade union or Congress officials, and the like. Chiefs therefore had become irrelevant and urban Africans had no need of them. Others took a more frankly hostile line: chieftainship was an outdated legacy of the past, an expression of 'tribalism' which impeded the emergence of a modern African nation. 'Let us do away with chiefs, and progress.' Curiously, one of those who spoke against the motion was a leading official of the African National Congress in Ndola. His was a pragmatic argument: chieftainship did retain meaning in the towns because, even though Africans were now urbanized, they still recognized that they belonged to different tribes. Others pointed to the valuable work by the Tribal Elders, regarded here as representatives of the chiefs, in settling disputes according to custom, and in this way reminding urban Africans of their cultural heritage. 'To do away with chiefs', one speaker pointed out, 'would be dangerous, for it would mean losing those traditions which every society should have.' The motion was very narrowly defeated.

Visits made by chiefs to the towns can provide valuable material for the further exploring of these questions, in particular as a way of measuring expressed attitudes against actual behaviour. Gutkind (1966), for example, in the course of a general discussion of the position of African urban chiefs refers to the visit of a Tembu chief to Cape Town reported by Mafeje. The visit apparently aroused violent opposition from many migrants to whom it appeared that 'chieftainship was an anachronism'. Chieftaincy in urban areas, Gutkind comments, following Mafeje, 'has to battle with the forces of westernization which have completely undermined the position of the chief and other tribal dignitaries'. In what follows I have presented some observations made on the Copperbelt which indicates that matters may be more complex than this formulation allows, and that there at least it would be dangerous to generalize on the basis of the response to one visit by one chief.

During April 1956 Chitmukulu, Paramount Chief of the Bemba, in the company of the District Commissioner, Kasama, and attended by other staff of the Bemba Native Authority, paid an official visit to the Copperbelt. His first public appearance in Ndola was at a football match in the municipal location. My friend Mkamba, as a senior official of the Copperbelt Football Association, was on hand to greet the chief and introduce him to the teams. When I ran into Mkamba a few days later he asked me whether I had seen Chitimukulu myself, and then went on without invitation to express his surprise at the chief's reception. 'Only the people from the west now give respect to their chiefs.' When the car bearing the chief arrived, he said, he himself had knelt down in greeting as an example to the others, but none had followed it. When he introduced the chief to the two teams the players had knelt down and clapped,[16] but as for the people gathered to watch the match they did not even stand up or raise their hats; they just looked at him as if he were an ordinary man. Meanwhile, one of my research assistants who was in the crowd as a spectator recorded some of the spontaneous comments heard around him. Most of these were in the kind of Bemba spoken in the towns which I have translated: 'In future no Bemba is going to talk down to me. Can this one here really be Chitimukulu? Why, he's dressed just like a Kalwena.' Or again: 'Is this the one for whom I was asked money as a gift for the chief? Not me — I shan't be going back to the villages. This one is a chief for the villagers, those who cut trees.'[17] One man speaking in English was heard to ask his companions whether they proposed to attend a ceremony of welcome for the chief after the match. One of his friends replied: 'What! Wasting my time on that. I have other things to do. I have no time for him.'

Later that evening a gathering was arranged at the house of one of the Bemba Tribal Elders. I heard from a number of different sources that the attendance was not large; some sixty to eighty on one estimate, most of whom were older people or who came from Lubemba itself, Chitimukulu's own area.

At Mufulira, the next stage on the chief's tour, the reception was even cooler. A van with a loud-hailer attachment had moved around the mine compound announcing the chief's arrival, and advising people where they should muster if they wished to greet him. In fact he was almost totally ignored, and he remained sitting in his van. A few Bemba passing by, noticing the uniformed District Messengers, asked whether a tax collection was in progress, and when informed that it was a visit of the chief one of them said:

'Those who want the chief can come and greet him. Here we are all our own chiefs, we all work for ourselves.' Shortly afterwards it was suggested that the chief should leave the van in order to meet at least the handful of people who had come to a nearby office. When two men gave him the royal salute, other Bemba around were heard muttering: 'Can one lie down on the ground like that when one is wearing clean clothes? Anyway, look at this chief — the way he wears his shirt. And not even a tie.' When shortly afterwards he returned to his vehicle there were no ululations from the women or other greetings that customarily mark the departure of a Bemba chief.

At first glance this account of Chitimukulu's visit to the Copperbelt might appear to lend strong support for the view offered by Mafeje based on the visit of the Tembu chief to Cape Town. Certainly many of the comments offered reflect a degree of westernization in the sense employed by Mafeje or of urbanization in Mayer's sense. Such a view, however, would fail to take account of the remarkable contrast between Chitimukulu's reception in 1956 and the almost rapturous welcome he received on a similar visit in 1952. On the earlier occasion it was as though the entire African population had turned out to greet him, lining the streets in their thousands along the entire route from the railway station to the location some three miles away. As one of my informants put it, the crowds were so dense that 'the Europeans were amazed and wondered what kind of King this was for whom so many people had turned out'. What lay behind this dramatic change?

As many analysts (e.g. Watson 1958) have shown, the position of a chief in a colonial regime is fraught with difficulty; in a situation of crisis marked by the opposition of Government and people, these difficulties are thrown into uncomfortable relief as the chief is torn between the demands of the colonial authorities, whose servant he is, and the expectations of his subjects. When Chitimukulu visited Ndola in 1952 he had just returned from London where, together with leaders of the African National Congress, he had sought to persuade the British Government not to proceed with its plans for a Central African Federation. By 1956 the Federation had come into being, Chitimukulu had come to terms with the new situation, and had broken with Congress. For many Africans on the Copperbelt it was as though he had turned his back on his own people, a view neatly summarized in the remarks of spectators at the football match: 'Look, mates, at the "informer" there coming with his brothers [i.e., the Europeans in the party]. See how they guard him in the middle.' Or again: 'There isn't in the whole country a chief as stupid as this one. All his fellow chiefs are in Congress, not he — Government tool!'

It is evident then that the kind of reception accorded to Chitimukulu in 1956 is not to be accounted for in terms of westernization or similar concepts. Nor, conversely, can the events of that visit be taken to prove that 'tribalism' was in decline. An episode that occurred at Kitwe on one of Chitimukulu's visits there provides a neat illustration of the point. The Chief's anti-Congress stance had aroused considerable displeasure on the Copperbelt, and near the Beer Hall an Ngoni man suddenly stepped up to Chitimukulu, proceeded to abuse him and finally slapped him and knocked him to the ground. This was grossly provocative behaviour and in ordinary circumstances might well have had serious consequences, including perhaps a prison sentence for the offender. The matter did go to the Urban Court, but it was held that the defendant's behaviour fell within the scope of the joking relationship that exists in towns between Bemba and Ngoni. It appeared later that the assault had actually been instigated by a Bemba. No Bemba could have expressed his feelings so strongly or directly without risk of heavy punishment. He was able to do so indirectly, however, by exploiting the *bunungwe* or joking relationship between the two groups, knowing that in this way the chief could not take umbrage, and would at the same time be apprised of his people's profound dissatisfaction.[18] But before seeking to carry further this discussion of the position of chiefs in relation to 'tribalism' and ethnic identity, it may be instructive to compare the last visit of Chitimukulu with that of Mwata Kazembe, Senior Chief of the Lunda in the Kawambwa District.[19]

Shortly after the news of the forthcoming visit of Kazembe was received, one of my research assistants, Chileya Chiwale, himself a Lunda, was visiting the Beer Hall where he ran into a group of his friends, all of them originally from Mwansabombwe, Kazembe's capital. They quickly turned to discussing the visit of the chief. 'A lot of rubbish', was the immediate comment of one man. 'Is he going to come with the Bwanas from Kawambwa in the way his fellow chief Capricorn Chiti came?'[20] The others however quickly rounded on him, and reproved him for talking in that way.

It would be a great day, they said, for Mwata would come with a team of dancers who would perform *cikwasa* and *cilumwalumwa*. Among other Lunda the news was greeted with some anxiety lest Kazembe's visit turned out to be the same fiasco as Chitimukulu's, but the prevailing mood was one of anticipation. 'It will be a day of great pride', said one woman.

Near the house of the Lunda Tribal Elder a special shelter had been erected for the chief. Here on the Saturday afternoon a great crowd gathered to see Kazembe, resplendent in *mukonzo* and *cibalika*, the ceremonial garb and head-dress, and to enjoy the spectacle. The whole area throbbed to the beating of the *cinkumbi* by a blind drummer of the chief's entourage. The excitement mounted as a troupe of maidens from the court at Mwansabombwe appeared to perform the *cikwasa* dance, and as the dance got under way the enthusiasm of the crowd was expressed in the ululations of the women and the clapping of the men. As the dance closed the girls knelt in salutation before Kazembe, and then the Urban Court member, himself garbed in the *mukonzo* and *cibalika* of a Lunda aristocrat, and armed with an *mpoko* sword, advanced towards the chief, pointed the sword in his face and began to recite *malumbo*, the praise names of the chief. The climax came when shortly afterwards two of the sons of Kazembe began to perform the dance known as *mutomboko*. People poured forward to push money into the hands and pockets of the dancers, while all around there was applause and shouts of acclamation. 'These Lunda are a clever lot. No wonder they are used to keeping themselves apart.' 'You see now', another was heard to remark to his companion, 'why one would not be ashamed to admit he was Lunda because this "tribe" is very "heavy", and their chief shows pride in himself,[21] not like our Chiti. Oh, that one is a nonentity [*uwa cabe*].' Another man, who appeared to be a Ndebele from Southern Rhodesia, said to his friend in English:

> 'Many people turned up today because they heard that the chief had come with drums and dancers; had it not been so there would have been very few here. But that is what an important chief should do. It is no good a chief coming to the Copperbelt where there are many different tribes and Europeans too and leaving behind his traditional things. He has to make people feel confidence and pride in him as an African chief. That is why

your Bemba chief was not respected. You Bemba say *ubufumu bucindika umwine*, chieftainship respects its owner. If you do not respect and have confidence in yourself, how can you expect others to respect you?'

A few days after Kazembe's departure[22] Chiwale ran into some of his friends at the market-place. All of them were Congress officials and they had come to arrange a meeting with the African Market Vendors' Association. They quickly fell into discussion of Kazembe's recent visit. One, a Bemba, said:

'The coming of your chief was very good because in this way it can show the Europeans the dignity and importance of African chiefs ... Chiefs are like our fathers and you know if a chief sent a message all over his area it would be followed. Therefore the Government has this in mind that if all chiefs are invested with power through tricks it would be able to break any organization in their areas just as the chiefs in the Gwembe Valley are doing now.'

Another supported this saying that had he known that Kazembe had recognized Congress in his area he would have arranged for a choir to sing for him in Ndola. Anyway, he concluded, everyone had admired Kazembe's visit and the way he had answered the Bwanas because that showed he was an African chief, and did not want to lose respect or demean the chieftainship in their eyes.[23]

I have reported these visits of chiefs to the Copperbelt at some length because they appear to me to illustrate well the complexities in the contemporary relationship between urban Africans and their traditional tribal leaders. In observing responses and reactions on these occasions we cannot help being made aware yet again of the many seeming contradictions which surround the whole issue of 'tribalism'. There can be no question that as a result of living in towns Africans have introduced and accepted many changes into their way of life; they are becoming more westernized; it is also plain that many have become urbanized in the sense employed by Mayer. What should also be patent is that such concepts are quite inadequate to account for the markedly different receptions accorded to Chitimukulu within such a short space of time; they fail even more woefully to explain why on his most recent tour Chitimukulu should have been almost completely ignored, not to say spurned, whereas Kazembe, whose visit made such explicit use of traditional cultural symbols, was greeted with much enthusiasm. A number of themes emerge from our account, each of which merits scrutiny.

Perhaps the first preliminary point that should be noted is the need to understand the attitudes and behaviour adopted towards a chief within its relevant social context. Under modern conditions, a chief operates within a number of fields of social relationships. Within his own tribal area he is the acknowledged ruler of his people, and his authority, while clearly dependent on the recognition and support of the colonial administration, still owes much to the customary definition and perception of his role. Then, in the field of Black-Black relations, he is the representative of his tribe, a symbol of its unity in opposition to other similar groups and categories. Finally, the chief also operates in the field of Black-White relations. This indeed is the crucial area, serving to define his position within the other fields of relationship. It is in this context, moreover, that he becomes a representative not only of his own tribespeople, but of all Africans; he becomes a symbol of African leadership in opposition to the Europeans. It is this fact which enables us to understand why, as mentioned earlier, chiefs may be rated highly on a social ranking scale by respondents belonging to groups in which chieftainship was not a highly developed indigenous institution. It is also this aspect of the chief's position which assumes dominance in the context of an official tour of the Copperbelt. I have mentioned how on the occasion when Kazembe himself was to dance, the location police had some difficulty in handling the crowd. There was much jostling and apparently some Lunda began throwing their weight around, much to the annoyance of the non-Lunda spectators. 'Is this your chief alone?', they protested. 'He didn't come just to see you.' The visiting chief, unless he is on a purely private trip, is received by the townspeople at large, and he is judged not simply as the representative of a particular tribe, but rather as an African chief. What becomes of crucial importance in this situation, therefore, is his record as a national spokesman, as the many references to Chitimukulu's vacillating relations with the African National Congress make clear.

Unfortunately, social behaviour is rarely to be explained by such simple formulae, and the differential responses to Chitimukulu's and Kazembe's visits cannot be fully accounted for in this way. For if it had been simply a matter of his overt political stance, Kazembe's reception would hardly have differed greatly from that of the Bemba Paramount. Kazembe, too, had had his recent brushes with Congress, and if it was the case that he had already mended his fences in that direction, news of this was evidently slow to reach the ears of Congress officials in Ndola, who would then have given him a formal welcome. Clues to some of the other factors at work are to be found in the spontaneous observations offered by bystanders and passers-by of the kind I have already cited. Many of the comments related to the dress and appearance of the chiefs. Thus Chitimukulu came in for much adverse criticism not only because he had deviated from the Congress line, but also because of his slovenly demeanour: 'he looks just like a Kalwena'. This was a reference to one of the groups from the far west who, as has been noted, provide most of the men for the town's night-soil removal service, and who are also held in low esteem for their poor and scruffy appearance. That Chitimukulu should have been referred to in these terms was thus not only highly derogatory, it also supports the point made earlier that negative attitudes towards a chief cannot be made the basis for inferences about the changing status of 'tribalism' among urban Africans. On the contrary, the judgment of Chitimukulu was made in terms of the urban categories, and in this respect confirms the view of 'tribalism' proposed by Mitchell as a set of categorical relationships. At the same time, as I have suggested, there is another aspect to 'tribalism' which is also revealed in the same speaker's remark: this is the image of the self which it discloses.

Mitchell has discussed fully in *The Kalela Dance* the importance that urban Africans attach to clothes. Western-style dress has come to serve as a symbol of the 'civilized way of life' associated with the dominant Europeans; that way of life in turn has provided a scale in terms of which the African urban population is stratified. Mitchell's interpretation of *Kalela*, with its exaggerated emphasis on proper attire, was that it represented the vicarious participation of unskilled and uneducated Africans in the civilized life-style of the African 'middle-class' to which they themselves aspired.[24] From this point of view Chitimukulu had shown himself to be 'uncivilized'; he had demeaned not only his person, but his position as an African chief, for by his deportment he earned Africans the contempt of the Europeans. By contrast, even though he was not dressed in the western fashion, Kazembe was highly acclaimed; garbed in his chiefly robes, he carried himself with dignity, and displayed his chieftainship as an institution in which Africans themselves could feel pride. Here was a chief, it was said, who by his comportment and presence would compel the respect of the Europeans. In this way, African self-respect was itself enhanced.

The response to the visits of the chiefs was thus also coloured by the bearing these had on people's sense of their identity as Africans. But for many, and particularly the Bemba and Lunda, there was also the bearing they had on their own sense of tribal identity. I shall take up the question of the Bemba in my second essay, and confine myself here to the position of the Lunda. For the latter, the visit of Kazembe was evidently an occasion of great excitement and satisfaction. They were able to enjoy the pleasure of watching *cikwasa* and thus to be reminded of their own cultural heritage, but no less important, it would seem, was the experience of having their claim to pride in being Lunda acknowledged in the acclamation accorded to Kazembe and his party by the people of other tribes. As one man was overheard to remark at the dancing: 'This is one of the main reasons why other tribes in the Kawambwa District like to regard themselves as Lunda; it is because of the superiority of the Namangungu, the Lunda proper.'

I have been suggesting then that 'tribalism' on the Copperbelt has to be looked at in two aspects: one, socio-centrically or 'objectively', as a system of social categories; and two, egocentrically or 'subjectively'. It is this second aspect one has in mind when one speaks of ethnic identity. Looking at the matter in this way, I believe, helps to account for some otherwise puzzling features of Copperbelt 'tribalism'. In the past, as I have mentioned, I sought to explain some of these seeming inconsistencies by invoking the principle of situational selection. In general, it seems to me, the material I have now presented confirms the value of that approach; what the present analysis adds, I believe, is a clearer understanding of the underlying mechanism at work. Thus what is important about a particular situation is not only the socially defined role that one occupies in it, but also the perception of self that one brings to it. Thus, once the distinction is made between 'tribalism' in its internal and external aspects, it becomes clearer how an individual can apply different criteria in perceiving himself and others. When, for example, a man like Mulenga thinks of himself his self-image is primarily that of an educated African of the 'middle-class'; when he refers to others, however, he is likely to resort to stereotypy, reflecting the 'external' system of tribal categories. Similarly, despite his own self-image, Mulenga may appear to others as 'a man who hates all Lozi'. Here, that is to say, his Bemba identity is 'imposed' upon him as it were from the outside; it does not coincide with his own perception of self.

Such a perspective may also be helpful in resolving other difficulties. Thus it might seem at first glance a curious phenomenon that 'tribalism' should flourish at the very time that tribal custom declines in significance as a regulator of behaviour. I have noted elsewhere (Epstein 1958:231) how in a 'tribal' regime the total body of custom provides the basis for those mutual expectations that are necessary to social intercourse. Within, say, Bembaland, even in today's conditions of change, there are still general guidelines enabling one to judge how people might behave in particular circumstances. On the Copperbelt, by contrast, to be told that a man is Bemba allows no inferences to be drawn about his likely conduct in different situations: he may continue to observe various customary practices where this is possible, or he may, like Mulenga, have little knowledge of them. Despite this, Africans on the Copperbelt do distinguish between individuals and categories in terms of what they call 'tribal consciousness'. By this they refer both to the intensity of interaction within particular categories, and to the continued attachment to customary practices and values said to be characteristic of such categories. Thus even before the coming of Kazembe I frequently heard Lunda spoken of as more 'tribalized' than others, even though to the outsider they appeared to be no less involved than others in the life of the town. This suggests that while the persistence of custom may be irrelevant so far as 'tribalism' in its categorical aspect is concerned, it may be of the utmost importance for individuals and groups in defining or helping to maintain their own ethnic identity.

The issues raised here are very much bound up with another major problem in regard to ethnicity: to understand the dynamics that feed and keep it in being or, alternatively, lead to its decline and perhaps disappearance. As Mayer suggests, to discuss 'tribalism' in categorical terms alone is likely to produce a static picture: we understand how the categories emerge, but little of what makes for movement once the system has come into being. Here again, I believe, the dual approach may prove useful because we can then study ethnicity as a process of interaction between 'objective category' and 'subjective identity' within a variety of social environments. Before taking up this aspect of the problem, however, we need to examine the workings of ethnicity in some other contexts.

\* \* \*

## Ethnic identity and social change in Melanesia

When they survey Melanesia, as a whole, anthropologists are commonly led to represent the region as a kind of crazy quilt or patchwork, revealing a pattern of 'geographically random and inexplicable diversity', as Lawrence and Meggitt (1965:9) have phrased it. Mainland Papua-New Guinea and the neighbouring islands have indeed provided a habitat over countless generations for many diverse peoples, occupying contrasting ecological settings, organized in highly fragmented societies, and speaking a myriad of tongues. In pre-colonial times political organization was universally on a small scale, and social life essentially parochial; nowhere throughout the entire region do we find centralized polities of the kind familiar, say, in many parts of Africa where large and often ethnically heterogeneous populations were bound together within the framework of a state and gave their allegiance to a powerful monarch or tribal chief. This situation is clearly reflected in the 'cognitive maps' produced by different indigenous groups: the boundaries are highly circumscribed and quickly shade into *terra incognita* (see, e.g. Burridge 1960:10).

But rapid and far-reaching changes have been taking place in New Guinea, particularly since the end of the Second World War, leading to a transformation of indigenous 'world-views', and in turn to the re-drawing of these 'cognitive maps'. For groups like the Kuma in the Western Highlands, for example, the social universe no longer comprises merely the divisions of clan, tribe, and phratry; as Marie Reay (1971:219) has noted recently, disputes in a public bar or on a plantation nowadays sort men by council area, by Sub-District and District, and even by broader regions where all Highlanders are linked in opposition to the peoples of the

Sepik or all of Papua. Such views find behavioural expression in the context of casual interaction, but they are also most important in more purely political situations. Thus summing up a study of the elections for the Papua-New Guinea House of Assembly in 1968, which revealed evidence of regional chauvinism in many parts of the country, Parker (1971:360) comments that if it was doubtful whether New Guinea politics were evolving toward the Westminster system of responsible government, it was even more uncertain whether they were in transition towards one polity or many. In a word, ethnicity appeared to be emerging as a potent factor in New Guinea politics in much the same way that 'tribalism' and 'regionalism' have done in Africa and elsewhere among the newly independent nations. How has this situation developed? In discussing 'tribalism' on the Copperbelt I was chiefly concerned with the operation of ethnicity in an urban context, and looked at it in overall perspective rather than from the vantage-point of any particular ethnic group. Here I adopt a different approach, and examine the situation from the perspective of a rurally-based group in adaptation to changing social conditions: my theme is the emergence of a Tolai ethnic identity.

*Village roots.* A number of recent studies of the Tolai are now available which have discussed in some detail the changes that have overtaken social life on the Gazelle Peninsula over the past hundred years. Here, therefore, I can review some of the processes at work in more summary form, though from a particular standpoint. My task will be to describe the ways by which Tolai became increasingly involved in the new colonial society created in Papua-New Guinea by the coming of the Whites, and to show how that process of involvement has affected their perception of themselves as individuals and as members of groups.

As elsewhere in Melanesia, pre-colonial Tolai society was organized on the basis of small, independent territorial units which the Tolai called *gunan* — villages or parishes, to use a term now frequently employed in the ethnographic literature of the region. The parish is defined in this context as the largest local group forming a political unit, but in fact the *gunan* in the past rarely functioned as a single solidary unit. Within the *gunan* fighting that might lead to homicide was proscribed, but where an attack was contemplated on another parish the *gunan* of the raiders did not necessarily participate as a whole; many would join the war-party only when they had received an assurance that they would have their reward in *tambu*, the local shell currency. Nevertheless, such fighting was perceived as an encounter between *gunan*, and in this sense the village provided a major category of inclusion/exclusion.

This remains the position even today. Primary identification is in terms of the village, and *gunan* identity serves as an organizing principle of behaviour in contexts where Tolai from different localities congregate together. At the Rabaul market, for example, the female vendors occupy pitches which have come to be associated with different villages, while at ceremonies people may be seen from time to time clustered or sitting together in village blocs.

Today, as in the past, some of the larger parishes are comprised of a number of smaller units, also known as *gunan*; these are made up in turn of tiny residential groups or hamlets. In everyday life the hamlets and sections of the village enjoy a high degree of autonomy, yet all are bound by common ties to the village and are expected to display solidarity, particularly in the face of other groups. An episode from the island of. Matupit where I myself worked, may be cited to illustrate the processes at work. There are today at Matupit three main village sections — Kurapun, Rarup, and Kikila — each of which has its own Councillor who represents it on the Gazelle Native Local Government Council.[25] Lineage elders within the various village sections control lands around the base of Matupi crater where the megapode or brush turkey deposits its eggs. The eggs are a valued part of the local diet, but they are also an important source of Matupi income in cash and *tambu*. For this reason the Kurapun 'owners' had at one point refused access to the people of Nodup, a neighbouring Tolai community, to collect eggs from their land. The Nodup were highly incensed, and it was reported that they intended to impose a taboo on their own lands so that no Matupi would be able to collect coral there for the production of slaked lime-powder.[26] Some time afterwards a man from Kikila, discovering that men from Kurapun were gathering eggs from his land without paying him the prescribed levy, forthwith forbade anyone from there collecting any more eggs. When this became known at the next public assembly in Kikila, the owner of the land was severely reprimanded by one of his fellow elders. 'It is true that we are known as Kikila, Rarup, and Kurapun.

But we call ourselves the people of Matupit. We are one island, we are Matupi. And what you have said, my friend, is not good, for you are dividing us, cutting us off from our brothers, our sisters and our matrikin in Kurapun.' One of the things that bothered the elder was that Kurapun might retaliate by refusing Kikila women access to land there where they were accustomed to growing certain vegetables and collecting firewood. As between Matupit and Nodup there were also bonds of economic interdependence but clearly, as one contributor to the discussion stated explicitly, one could not treat the people of Kurapun as one could the people of Nodup. The owner of the egg-lands was required to go and make his apologies to the people of Kurapun, and to remove the ban forthwith.

The *gunan* then was a territorial unit. As I have mentioned, however, each village or village section was made up of a number of small, and often scattered, hamlets. The land of each hamlet was associated with a particular descent group or *vunatarai*. Thus a *gunan* would be composed of many different descent groups; in the terminology of Hogbin and Wedgwood (1953), Tolai parishes were multi-carpellary. Unlike the village, however, the local descent group was not a bounded and spatially discrete unit; its members were linked by ties of kinship and clanship with people in many other local communities. Crucial in this regard was the regulation of marriage. Sexual relations and hence marriage were forbidden with certain close categories of kin, but the rule of exogamy was carried primarily by the moiety system. Tolai society was built up around a dual division, so that every Tolai belonged by way of descent to one or other moiety. Different names attached to the moieties in different parts of the area, but since regular correspondences were also recognized, in fact a uniform system operated within the Tolai area, the neighbouring Duke of York Islands, and parts of southern New Ireland. The moieties possessed no internal organization; they constituted descent categories in the strict sense. Apart from their role in the regulation of marriage, they also provided Tolai with a ready means of conceptualizing in a simple way their complex universe of social and political relations. In this regard the moieties provided a second major category of inclusion/exclusion, well illustrated in the fact that in everyday social intercourse people often referred to the moieties not by name but simply as *'Avet'* and *'Diat'*, the 'we-folk' and the 'they-folk'.[27]

Yet it must be stressed that the Tolai in former times were not a unified group; lacking a common historical tradition, they lacked too a common identity. Relations between parishes were marked by suspicion and hostility, and inter-village raiding and warfare occurred frequently. On the other hand, relations between Tolai groups were qualitatively different from those which obtained between Tolai and a number of other peoples who were autochthonous to the area: the Bainings, the Taulil, the Sulka, and Butum. Warfare among Tolai was governed by convention, and the transfer of *tambu* provided a customarily recognized way of making peace. The Tolai raided the other groups for slaves, and had gradually pushed them from their areas of settlement further and further inland.[28] However, Tolai groups were also cross-linked in a variety of ways. In the first place there was an intricate network of marriage ties criss-crossing the area; thus they shared in a common gene pool. Second, there were the important links forged through participation in shared institutions: for example, shell-money which played a central role in secular as well as religious and ceremonial life — as a medium of exchange in all commercial transactions, as a means of making reparation for wrongs, as the only acceptable form of marriage-payment, and as essential to the activities associated with the cult of the *dukduk* and *tubuan*. Finally, there was the factor of language: dialectal variation was important, but did not appear to provide a barrier to communication between groups, though here again it must be remembered that the contemporary homogeneity of tongue owes a great deal to the efforts of the missionaries. It seems clear then that if in pre-colonial times there was no sense of common identity among the different Tolai communities, there were at least the seeds of one, based on a variety of shared understandings and values. The imposition of alien rule, the new social environment that this created, in particular the extension of the boundaries of their social universe to include peoples hitherto unknown, provided the conditions in which these seeds could germinate.

*Autonomy and dependence.* However varied in their approach to identity psychoanalysts are, there appears to be general consensus that at its core lies the issue of self-esteem. Thus, discussing the beginnings of ego-identity, Erikson (1963:235) refers to a child learning to walk. The internalization of a particular version of 'one who can walk', he observes, is one of the many steps in child development each of which, when successfully achieved, contributes to a more realistic self-esteem. 'This self-esteem grows to be a conviction that one is learning effective steps towards a tangible future, and is developing into a defined self within a social reality.' Closely linked, then, with self-esteem is the notion of autonomy, the capacity to master one's environment and to express oneself in ways that win the approval of those who most immediately surround one. Crucial in the earliest stages of the development of ego-identity, scope for autonomous expression remains as a basic personality need throughout life.

Identity formation, then, is intimately bound up with the social context within which the person grows up and matures. From this point of view the coming of the Whites to New Guinea had profound implications, because once a population comes under alien rule opportunities for the display of autonomy in customary ways may be changed quite radically. As I have discussed elsewhere (Epstein 1971), the colonial situation brings into being a new scheme of relationships of dependence. This is most immediately evident in the arena of power relationships or politics. Thus new offices, carrying powers and responsibilities of a kind unknown to the indigenous system, may be introduced or recognition be accorded in varying degree to traditional leaders; in either event the incumbents are in a position of tutelage. But dependence is not confined to the field of political relations; it permeates and affects almost every facet of social life. Dependence, however, is not uniform in its consequences for different groups and categories within the colonized population; alien dominance can allow of a considerable degree of autonomy in political as well as other contexts, and hence of continuity with the past. Within the limits and framework of the changed social environment, individuals and groups may continue to pursue traditionally sanctioned goals and purposes, and deploy customary resources to these ends. Adaptation to the changed circumstances is thus bound up with the possibilities for the continuing exercise of autonomy, the capacity to redefine the new situation in terms of established meanings and values.

It is interesting to compare early Tolai reactions to the new developments with those of other groups in New Guinea. Thus one

early observer, Baessler (1895:104), has recorded the unwillingness
of local people, both in New Britain and on the mainland, to work
on the plantations, so that foreign labour had to be imported, but
he also notes the greater keenness of the former to trade their
produce. Blum (1900:139) contrasts even more sharply the behaviour of the people around Madang who planted hardly enough
fruits, vegetables, and bananas to meet their own household needs
with that of 'the enterprising trading people of the Gazelle Peninsula' who took advantage of the European demand for yam, taro,
and bananas and planted these vegetables and fruits 'in abun-
dance'.

In New Guinea, as in other colonial territories, the use of
migrant labour was a principal means of integrating indigenous
peoples into the modern cash and wage economy. And although
Tolai too sold their labour, the fertility of their soils, the greatly
extended market created by the coming of the Whites and the
opening of plantations, and the fact that producing crops to
acquire wealth was a basic feature of their traditional culture,
enabled them to participate in the labour market on a much more
restricted scale than other New Guineans.

In addition to increasing their production of foodstuffs, the
Tolai also responded favourably to official encouragement to
increase their plantings of coconut palms. Hence, within a fairly
short time, they had come to participate in the growing prosperity
of their area, and were beginning to establish closer links with the
wider society. The experience of colonialism was bringing about
many important changes in their way of life, but the important
point that needs to be stressed at this stage is that it did not entail a
radical dislocation of the pre-existing system of social relationships
and the scheme of values that went with it. On the contrary, far
from undermining the traditional system, current developments
served to buttress it at a number of important points. Tolai
involvement in the new colonial society was mediated chiefly
through the land; the land not only continued to meet their
requirements for subsistence, it was also the major source of their
new wealth. The character of the palm, on which this wealth was
founded, is important in this context. Because of its longevity, the
palm was required to be planted only on land to which one could
claim entitlement as a member of the 'owning' descent group or
*vunatarai*; rights of control over land vested in these groups in

perpetuity. Thus rights to land not only continued to be regulated by customary rules of tenure, but were also dependent on the continuing fulfilment of kinship obligations. All this in turn served to perpetuate forms of political authority based on control and administration by big men and elders of their lineage lands. *Luluais*, the new government appointed village headmen, acquired duties and responsibilities that were no part of the customary role of the *ngala*. Yet for the reasons just mentioned the *luluai* continued to display many of the characteristic attributes of the traditional 'big man'. In the process of adaptation to their new circumstances the Tolai were thus able to maintain a considerable degree of continuity with their past.

Autonomy makes for positive identity. We also have to take account of elements in the situation making for negative identity. Adjustment to dependence ushers in what may be termed the paternalist phase in the colonial experience. The phase is chiefly characterized by a vast social gulf that separates the indigenes from their new masters. This has two main consequences. In the first place, having been subdued by the colonials' overwhelming command of power, the indigenes experience a return to an infantile condition of powerlessness; they themselves, and their institutions, are deemed to be without dignity or value. On the other hand, as Mannoni (1956:80*ff*) stresses, the dependency relationship also has a strong bilateral component: it gives rise to claims on the part of the dependants for whom it becomes a source of security. Among other things, this means that they come to perceive their governors as father-surrogates, powerful figures to be propitiated, respected, and obeyed, but who are at the same time seen as having assumed responsibility for protecting and providing for the needs of their wards.

Some of these processes are to be seen at work among the Tolai. Here it was not so much the Administration as the Christian missionaries who played the major part in seeking to undermine Tolai self-esteem. Their ancestors, they were taught, had lived in 'an age of darkness' (*ta ra e na bobotoi*), and the customs and practices they had bequeathed to their descendants were held up as the mark of godlessness and savagery. In his early ethnographic account the Roman Catholic missionary Kleintitschen (1906) presents the Tolai as a people possessed of few redeeming features, but according to Parkinson (1907:573) it was the Wesleyan

Methodists who were particularly intolerant of indigenous ways, all of which had to be extirpated in order to make way for Christianity. There are many possible responses to this situation. A familiar one is by way of what psychoanalysts call identification with the aggressor, meaning in this context the taking over by Tolai of many of the criteria of their overlords in evaluating themselves, their institutions, and their behaviour. This is what numbers of Tolai did, particularly those in the villages closest to Rabaul, adopting many of the more overt ways of the Whites. Matupit appears to have been particularly notable in this regard. According to Bürger (1923:154), since the Matupi earned a lot of money they were able to spend a great deal on clothes. 'They wore jackets and trousers, and if they wanted to dress up especially, they even wore collar and tie.' Many years later, when I was myself in the field, Matupi were often quick to point out that they had always been in the van of cultural innovation.

The adoption of western ways in regard to clothes or other consumer goods was not simply a matter of gaining status in the eyes of the dominant Whites. Since such purchases were only made possible by their wealth they served to distinguish and to differentiate coastal Tolai from those inland, but even more from the other New Guineans who had come as migrant labourers to the Gazelle Peninsula. Among the first Melanesians from outside the Gazelle with whom the Tolai came into contact were men from Buka, brought in by Parkinson, and used by him as a kind of personal police force.[29] How far this early experience with the Buka may have affected their perception of, and so their relations with, other indigenous groups, it is now impossible to say. Nor indeed is there much information available on early Tolai interaction with those New Guineans who were coming in increasing numbers from different parts of the country to work on the plantations of the Gazelle or in the township of Rabaul. Nowadays Tolai employ the word *a vok* (from Melanesian pidgin) to refer derogatorily to all of these foreign migrants. The term itself simply means a labourer, but it also evokes the image of a menial poorly and untidily attired in shorts and a shirt (usually torn), which was in marked contrast to the standard dress of Tolai males at this time — the *lavalava* or Samoan loincloth, which was also worn tailored for 'dress' occasions. The expression *vok* thus accurately reflected the Tolai view of the status differences between themselves and others. When the term first acquired currency I cannot say, but it is clear that there has been a tendency going back for many years for Tolai to see themselves as set apart from other groups. When conducting a study of the Maenge, another New Britain people living further to the south, Panoff (1969) found that many of his informants had worked on the Gazelle Peninsula in the 1920s. They described the reluctance of Tolai to show hospitality towards them, and said that foreign labourers were seldom, if ever, invited to festivals held in Tolai villages.

We have seen earlier how on the Copperbelt 'tribalism' emerged in response to the intermingling of peoples from many different backgrounds. In New Guinea the increasing mobility of people as they made their way to distant labour centres was generating a similar process. But in New Guinea 'tribal' groups were often too small and fragmented to provide the basis for meaningful categories, and instead 'territory' came to serve this end. Thus at the time of the Rabaul Strike in 1929, when all New Guineans employed in the town suddenly withdrew their labour, category terms such as Sepiks, Finschhafens, and the like seem to have become part of current usage. (Within the category, however, individuals associated on a linguistic or *wantok* — a term in Melanesian pidgin meaning those who speak the same language — basis, in much the same way as 'home-boys' did on the Copperbelt.) I have not been able to establish when the expression Tolai first came into use as a group designation. In the vernacular (which Tolai simply refer to as *tinata tuna*, the true or proper tongue) the word is used as a form of greeting or term of address, like 'mate' or 'comrade' in other cultures, when one does not know or prefers not to use the other's personal name. The earliest reference to it as a category term that I have been able to find in the written sources occurs in an item in the *Rabaul Times* contributed by a correspondent in Wau in 1936.[30] Although the usage may by this time have become well-established, the context suggests plainly that it was a product of the commingling of people from many different parts of the country brought about by the demand for labour in the New Guinea goldfields. In this instance, however, instead of making use of a territorial or locality name, a distinctive item of behaviour was seized upon to delineate the category; in time the term became completely accepted by the Tolai themselves.

We have in this case an excellent illustration of the interaction of external and internal perceptions in the development of ethnic identity. The group designation itself was the work of outsiders but the Tolai adopted it as their own because, presumably, serving in a context of polyethnic interaction as a useful signalling device, it also aptly expressed their awareness of the bonds that drew them together and separated them from others. Feeding into this nascent sense of ethnic identity was not simply an appreciation of their own cultural distinctiveness; there was also a heightened consciousness of shared experience following the imposition of alien rule and of their own position of advantage within the wider colonial society.

I have mentioned that in earlier days few Tolai offered their labour to the plantations; they could maintain their economic independence, and enjoy some degree of prosperity by continuing to stay at home and work the land. The vast majority of labourers on the plantations were thus recruited from elsewhere. During the thirties numbers of Tolai did seek work in Rabaul itself, but, according to contemporary reports and the data I was later to collect at Matupit, most of them showed a clear preference for 'free' casual employment as domestic servants, boat-boys, and laundrymen. Such an arrangement suited the Tolai admirably, for they could continue to live at home in the nearby villages; it was less attractive to European employers who frequently found cause to complain of 'native unreliability'. The fact was, of course, as the *Rabaul Times* (August 25, 1936) once ruefully acknowledged, that loss of, or dismissal from, employment held no terrors for the Tolai because every one was a landed proprietor. From this point of view it was, in a sense, the Tolai who were exploiting Rabaul: they used it as a market-place and as a source of employment for augmenting their cash-income from time to time, as well as for the other diversions the township offered; but they were not integrated into an urban system. Tolai recall the inter-war period as one in which they were subjected to many indignities: under the Native Regulations then in force they were subject to curfew within the township and were forbidden to wear European-style clothing;[31] they were also likely to be charged with theft if found in possession of bank-notes. [32] Even so, it is plain that they enjoyed a degree of autonomy and opportunities for meaningful achievement that were not available to most other indigenous groups.

Proximity to Rabaul offered a number of other advantages

besides opportunities for casual employment. As the major port and administrative centre of the Mandated Territory, Rabaul was at the hub of all social and economic development. An important by-product of this, for example, lay in regard to the provision of schooling. Thus many Tolai received training in the first technical school in the country started at Malaguna in the early twenties. In the mid-thirties, seemingly in response to pressure from the Tolai, the Administration set up the first Government school, the Waterhouse Memorial School at Nodup, which was to have a profound influence in later years. Finally, we should note here that Rabaul also provided the headquartes of the various missionary societies active in the Bismarck Archipelago, and their training institutions were also, therefore, located there. Given the nature of local conditions, the missions had been compelled to adopt a policy of working through indigenous catechists who were posted to the different villages in the area; but many on the completion of their training were sent out as teachers and 'missionaries' to more remote parts. Tolai were in the van of this movement, and Chowning (1969) has described the influence the teacher-'missionaries' were able to wield as emissaries of Tolai culture. For this reason, even today in some of these plaçes, Tolai are not seen so much as 'fellow natives' but as 'white men with brown skins'.

The economic development of the Gazelle Peninsula, the homogeneity of its people in regard to language and culture, and the headstart which the Tolai had acquired over other groups in the field of education were to contribute together, and in their several ways, to significant further advances following the Second World War. During the war itself the Gazelle was under Japanese military occupation, and the Tolai suffered grievously: many were killed by the Japanese, others died from malnutrition or lack of adequate medical supplies, while yet others perished in Allied bombing attacks. They also suffered material loss, for many of their coconut plantations — the major source of their wealth in cash — were destroyed, while in some communities accumulated stocks of shellmoney were seriously depleted. However, the end of the war saw the restoration of Australian rule to Papua-New Guinea, and before long there was evidence of a dramatic switch in the direction of policy from the negative approach that had characterized their administration in the inter-war years. This was seen in the adoption of a number of programmes for development in the economic and political fields as well as in health and education. One of the first major fruits of the new policy, aimed at stimulating and diversifying indigenous economic activities, was the setting up of the Tolai Cocoa Project in the early 1950s. The venture proved attractive to the Tolai, and gradually cocoa came to rival copra as a source of cash income (see T.S. Epstein 1968:51). In this same period the first official steps towards the establishment of representative political institutions in the Territory were being taken with the introduction on the Gazelle Peninsula of Native Local Government Councils. Initially, five councils were established there; and although in several areas local groups refused to participate in the new administrative arrangements, the amalgamation of the existing councils in 1963 to form the Gazelle Local Government Council was a clear expression of Tolai recognition of their area as a single community and their heightened sense of group identity. A no less important factor in the development of Tolai ethnic consciousness was the changing character of their involvement in the labour market. Before the war, as we have seen, many sought casual employment in Rabaul and some, too, had gone to work on the goldfields on the New Guinea mainland. In the post-war years, however, this situation was completely transformed with the emergence of a significant category of Tolai 'white-collar' workers, mainly teachers and clerks, many of whom were posted to stations throughout Papua-New Guinea.[33] There were also artisans, skilled carpenters, and mechanics who would find employment or win contracts for jobs in other parts of the country where local men of the required degree of skill were not yet available. Even when they joined the Constabulary or the Pacific Islands Regiment, Tolai appeared to enjoy an atypical status. So, for example, all the Matupi, of whom I have record, who joined the Police were employed as sergeant interpreter/clerks, or drivers, or belonged to the Police Band. In short, Tolai who were abroad in the early sixties stood out as an occupational elite, keenly aware that they were working in areas and among people much less advanced than their own.

Tolai identity in this period was affected not only by their status *vis-à-vis* other indigenous groups, but also by the changing character of their relations with the Europeans in their midst. Growing Tolai prosperity had profound implications for local commerce and business, and the more blatant forms of discrimination to which they had been subjected in the pre-war years gave way before the now substantial power of the Tolai purse. Non-monetary considerations were also present. As a result of the war there had been an almost complete turnover of the expatriate White population in and around Rabaul. Many of the category known locally as 'befores' died following the Japanese occupation and others departed; the new arrivals were mostly young people who did not share the 'white supremacist' attitudes of their predecessors. So the way was open, for example, for Tolai participation in the local cricket and baseball leagues, a development that would have been unthinkable to the European residents of pre-war Rabaul; personal friendships also began to spring up between individual Tolai and young Australians.

All of these developments produced, and at the same time expressed, a new-found confidence, a heightened self-esteem among the Tolai which was particularly striking to someone like myself who had earlier worked in another country of White settlement in Central Africa. There was, however, another side to the coin. Already during my first period of fieldwork there were evident signs of strain in the Tolai social system (Epstein 1961b). Land lay at the core of the problem, and it was becoming apparent that adjustments that had been possible a generation before were so no longer. With improved hospital and medical facilities, population growth was of quite staggering proportions.[34] Meanwhile, at the very moment that pressure on land was being intensified by the sheer increase in numbers, there was a heightened clamour for more land sparked off by the increased planting of coconuts and the introduction of a new cash crop in the form of cocoa. Nor was it simply that the supply of land was becoming inadequate to the demand. For it was precisely in these circumstances that the persistence of the customary system of land tenure, hitherto an important factor in the continuity and stability of Tolai social life, began to emerge as a source of irritation and a target for attack.

I have examined this situation in detail in my book *Matupit* (1969) and discuss there some of its implications, in particular the antagonism that was being generated between lineage elders, who provided the effective leadership within the village, not least because they continued to exercise control over the land, and a growing body of their landless sons. I have also shown how the emergence of an important category of 'white-collar' and urban workers fed into this cleavage and further exacerbated it. The two generations appeared increasingly to be pulled apart by different sets of interests, values, and attitudes. At the same time, the position of each was also marked by internal contradictions. Thus from time to time the younger men in wage employment would round upon the elders, accusing them of failure to discharge their obligations in the customary fashion in exercising their rights of control over land. On the other hand, for many of these same people the village no longer provided a meaningful arena in which to compete for prestige and prominence. Many of them, too, had become critical of the Local Government Councils, which they regarded as unrepresentative in their composition and, more importantly, as lacking any effective decision-making power. Linked to the wider society in more complex ways than their fathers, they had come to recognize that solutions to many of their more urgent problems were not to be found at the local level, and some were beginning to voice demands for more direct participation in the territorial political arena. A few went even further in linking their problems and the slowness of advance, to their continued state of political dependence, and one heard raised publicly for the first time the question of self-government for Papua-New Guinea. In order to elucidate these processes and tensions now at work, and their bearing on Tolai identity, I discuss below some aspects of the elections for the Papua-New Guinea House of Assembly in 1968 and the subsequent emergence of the Mataungan movement.

### The crisis of Tolai identity

It was a man from Matupit, Epineri Titimur, who first signalled the coming changes in the political climate of the Gazelle Peninsula. At a meeting of Tolai with the Territory's Administrator Sir Donald Cleland in Rabaul in 1961, Epineri pointed out that the Australians had been administering the country for close on fifty years, and then proceeded to ask when the people of Papua-New Guinea were to achieve self-government. When back at Matupit Epineri was taken publicly to task for his brashness in raising the matter without first consulting his fellows in the village, he explained that his intention was to sound 'a word of awakening' (*a tinata na tavagun*). And despite the fact that at the time he enjoyed little popular support, even within his own village, it appeared to the observer even then that Epineri's intervention in the discussion represented a watershed; henceforth one could expect to see a struggle develop between those who were prepared to seek change and a solution to current difficulties with the guidance of, and in co-operation with, the Administration, and those who, adopting a more militant stance, would demand more far-reaching changes, proceeding at an increased tempo, and a greater say in controlling their own destiny.

The elections for the recently established House of Assembly in 1964 provided some evidence in support of this expectation, but it was far from conclusive (see Polansky 1965). However, by the time the elections came round for the second House the situation on the Gazelle had crystallized further, and the pattern of development was much more clear-cut. The clash of attitudes and viewpoints on the direction of political development was expressed in the platforms advanced by the various candidates, the arguments they presented at campaign meetings, as well as in the comments and reactions of the electorate. A full account of the election has been published elsewhere (Epstein *et al.* 1971). Here, therefore, I need only touch briefly on some of the material relating to public attitudes towards the question of self-government and independence for Papua-New Guinea.

An immediate difficulty beclouding public discussion of these issues was the fact that the Tolai commonly used one vernacular term to cover both notions; the matter was further obscured by a widespread tendency to interpret independence as meaning not only the end of the Australian administration, but also the departure of all Europeans from the country. For many this was a frightening prospect. The following was a fairly typical comment:

'There are some people who are in a hurry. But see, there are not enough people who are sufficiently educated to govern the country properly. Perhaps in the years to come young people will have acquired a proper education, but at the moment there are few. Everything we have at present, everything that is provided is the work of Government. If the Government were to leave there would be great conflict and confusion. Who would govern us properly? See how often we Tolai start businesses. We work through the *turguvai* [a form of joint enterprise or partnership], but no sooner does it start then the parties to it are quarrelling among themselves, and then the whole thing collapses.'

Others who spoke in similar terms also referred to the likelihood of complete economic breakdown, even of the possibility of a return to fighting between groups in areas of the Gazelle that had been long pacified. Throughout such comments the Administration appeared primarily as playing the benevolent role of guardian. On the other hand, certain of these expressions of viewpoint also revealed a strong current of ambivalence. Thus one elder from an inland parish spoke of the many different regimes they had had in New Guinea; as one departed another came to take its place. He then went on to recall with bitterness how when the last war came the Australians 'had run away, leaving the people to die like sheep'. He talked as though the Administration was now planning another act of betrayal, leaving them defenceless against external aggression. Such views of course are an almost perfect expression of the dependency or paternalistic syndrome described by Mannoni, an important aspect of which, and one of the most powerful sources of fear and resentment, is the threat of abandonment. Those who held them were anxious to maintain their status of political dependence, at least for some time to come, happy in the degree of autonomy and the opportunities for self-expression that the system allowed them.

There were others, however, represented in the Rabaul electorate by Epineri Titimur, and in the adjoining constituency of Kokopo by a young man called Oscar Tammur, who were pressing for an end to the *status quo*. Epineri's precise stance was somewhat equivocal; to his opponents he appeared to stand out as an advocate of early independence, and they harped on this in an attempt to discredit him. To his own immediate supporters the matter appeared in a rather different light; he was not arguing for early independence so much as seeking to generate a change in the climate of opinion on the Gazelle. As one man from Matupit put it: 'It is not a question of independence to-morrow, but a proper preparation for it now, so that if it should come in five years we should be ready for it.' The fuller account of the election that is given in *Under the Volcano* shows that Epineri's support did not depend simply on his advocacy of political independence for Papua-New Guinea, and it may even be, as Parker (1971:330) suggests, that Epineri won not because of these views but in spite of them. Nevertheless, Epineri's vistory, and that of the youthful Tammur at Kokopo, did point to a significant shift in attitudes within the Tolai community, suggesting that they were at last beginning to emerge from the paternalist phase in their colonial history.

For many of the younger and more educated Tolai behind the desire for an end to political dependence was the drive for a greater measure of autonomy. But autonomy for whom and towards what end? I have referred earlier to autonomy as a basic personality need of the maturing individual. But just as the developing personality requires the capacity to relate to a widening range of persons, which later finds its expression in identification with a group or groups, so the drive for autonomy also has a social dimension: one seeks autonomy for the group with which one identifies. In some regards younger Tolai appeared to be reaching out towards a new identity as New Guineans, but they also revealed a deep concern for their position as Tolai within the proposed new polity. Some of the ambiguities in the situation are well brought out in the 'platform' of another of the candidates for election at Rabaul, Samson ToPatiliu. ToPatiliu was in many ways fairly representative of the new class of 'westernized' Tolai beginning to emerge on the Gazelle. Educated first at the Waterhouse Memorial School at Nodup and then in Australia, and now employed in the broadcasting service, ToPatiliu had lived for some time prior to the election among Europeans in one of the more select parts of Rabaul before moving back to Nodup. Yet ToPatiliu was also highly conscious of himself as a Tolai, and avowed a strong attachment to Tolai culture, one of his hobbies being to tape-record, and so preserve, the ancient songs of the *tubuan* and other ceremonies now disappearing. Part of his printed hand-out (in English) had this to say:

'Unless people of every language group are able to come together for the advancement of the country we will not have here Government of the People by the People, but government by some group. And what group will that be? It will certainly not be government by the Tolai.

But we Tolai are the most wealthy group in the country. It must be government by a less wealthy group, and I fear that they may want to spread our wealth around.'

A similar Janus-like stance characterized the Mataungan Association which sprang into being in 1969, and rapidly polarized Tolai society into two opposed camps. The initial purpose of the sponsors of the Association was to mobilize Tolai opposition to the Gazelle Multi-Racial Council with which the Administration proposed to replace the former all Tolai Gazelle Local Government Council, but Mataungan quickly developed into a fully-fledged political movement, establishing its own organs of administration and to some extent providing an alternative form of government in those areas which gave it support. At the Waigani Seminar, held at the University of Papua-New Guinea in Port Moresby in May 1970 one of the papers presented was by a young Tolai from Matupit, John Kaputin, an official spokesman for Mataungan, who spoke about some of its aims, in particular its approach to economic development. Kaputin presented himself as a New Guinean. 'The sense of being a New Guinean or Papuan is running more deeply and more passionately than many of you people realize', he said, 'and this new nationalist orientation is given additional fever by grinding itself in the yet more primitive and powerful awareness of being members of a disprivileged race.' Kaputin, however, also spoke as a Tolai, and the plans he unfolded were primarily for the Tolai, whom he hoped would 'set a prelude for a national movement in Papua-New Guinea'.

Kaputin spoke of Mataungan as representing all Papuans and New Guineans on the Gazelle, and there were reports at the time of Sepik labourers there forming their own branch of the Association, but in its origins and concerns it was, and remained, essentially a Tolai movement. Its position on the council question was unwavering: a demand for a return to the *status quo ante* and the re-establishment of an all Tolai body.[35] Mataungan aims were as much economic as political, and here too there was evidence of 'separatist' thinking. Thus one possibility that was being seriously canvassed was to bring home all those Tolai employed in more responsible jobs outside the Gazelle to help in the development of their own area. Finally, one may mention here an incident that brings out well the affective dimension in the situation. A number of Mataungan had been arrested and prosecuted on a charge of stealing the keys of the Council House. This was a purely symbolic gesture, conceived as part of the protest against the opening of the new Multi-Racial Council. Following the discharge of the defendants, a big party was organized at Matupit at which the guest of honour was an African lawyer on the faculty of the University at Port Moresby who had conducted the defence. To celebrate the victory there was a performance, all the more significant because so many years had elapsed since it was last seen at Matupit, of a *kinavai*, a central and dramatic feature of the ceremonies associated with the *dukduk* and *tubuan*; for this event a number of *tubuans*, or masked dancers, appeared at Matupit from many different parts of the Tolai area.

We are now in a better position to appreciate the crisis of identity which currently appears to be confronting many Tolai. As the process of social change has gathered momentum, the Tolai have become involved in increasingly complex ways in the wider society of Papua-New Guinea. This has been accompanied by two inter-related developments particularly noticeable in a community like Matupit. Already at the time of my first visit there was evidence among younger Matupi of a growing awareness of themselves as citizens of a new nation that was yet to come into being. Coupled with this was a loosening of the ties with one's local group and a declining attachment to the ways of the village which had contributed so much to the formation of Tolai identity. The emergence of that identity was itself a response to changing social circumstances. The transition to a national identity, however, is a much more complex process, beset by many obstacles.

I have noted how for a number of years many young Tolai men and women have been employed in relatively skilled and responsible jobs not only in the capital, Port Moresby, but throughout the entire country. In this way, in work and leisure, they have established common bonds, including the bonds of marriage, with other New Guineans. From their point of vantage, then, one might assume that many of them would come to see their futures set within this wider territorial framework. And this is indeed occurring, reflecting a growing identification with the nascent new nation. However, a counter-process is also at work. For, by a kind of paradox, the same forces for change, serving to generate this new sense of nationality, also operates to intensify the sense of Tolai identity and separateness.

The present conflict is revealed in a variety of contexts. Tolai, we have seen, had quickly come to stand out as an occupational elite within the country. But now, with a general improvement in educational standards throughout New Guinea, Tolai dominance in this field is increasingly threatened. Employment thus comes to be seen as an area of inter-ethnic competition. Again, Tolai abroad become keenly aware of the relative affluence of the Gazelle and the other advantages it enjoys over so many other parts of the country. Most, therefore, are anxious to get back there as quickly as they can. Moreover, as far as is possible, those who are away from home seek to maintain their rights in land, and many take advantage of a home-leave to plant cash-crops, which will be cared for in their absence by a kinsman, and will be a source of income in later years. Awareness of their relative affluence also makes them quick to perceive any threat to their position of advantage. Thus, during the 1968 elections speakers at village meetings constantly referred to the continuing subsidy of education in Papua by the Administration, whereas on the Gazelle these expenditures were met by the Local Government Council. Others again would point to the growth of urban centres like Port Moresby and Lae while Rabaul apparently was being allowed to stagnate. Clearly there was a strong feeling around that the Tolai were being mulcted in order to finance developments elsewhere.

Like the 'tribes' on the Copperbelt, then, the Tolai have become a category within a wider field of interaction (cf. Mitchell 1956:30). Moreover, because of the uneven development of the country as a whole, that field has become increasingly an arena in which different ethnic or regional groups seek to protect and advance their political and economic interests. Sensitivity to these issues grows out of, and in turn reinforces, the chronologically prior and now powerfully rooted perception of self provided by Tolai ethnic identity. Before the coming of the Whites, as I have sought to show, politically autonomous villages were nevertheless so cross-cut by many common bonds that the Tolai quickly came to see themselves as a distinctive group in contrast to other peoples with whom they were now brought into contact. That sense of identity was intensified by the peculiar position of advantage they came to enjoy within the colonial society of New Guinea, and the opportunities it provided for the exercise of personal and local autonomy. Change thus allowed for a considerable measure of continuity with the past. In these circumstances there was no marked incompatibility between the older, village-based identity and the more recently adopted ethnic one; the one 'nested' within the other and the two became mutually supportive. By contrast, the transition to a national identity allows of no such continuity, and is in fact accompanied, at least for the present, by sharp conflicts of interest. Moreover, the new entity with which one seeks to identify is still obscure in its outlines; the momentum towards nationhood is generated not so much by awareness of positive common bonds as by opposition to the colonialists. Elsewhere I have sought to present a view of change as proceeding through a process of involvement. By this I referred to the ways whereby, and the extent to which, a formerly autonomous group came to participate in wider fields of social interaction than was previously possible. Involvement here implies the continuous exercise of choice among an increased range of alternatives. Such choices, of course, are made within a framework of constraint and once made set up further demands and impose new constraints. From this perspective the adoption of a new national identity is itself a matter of choice, but it is also a choice in which conscious motives appear to play an important part. Under contemporary conditions the decision to remain a Tolai also reflects a conscious choice, but it is one that is more likely to be affected by a rich store of unconscious associations and identifications. Growing out of a certain set of social conditions Tolai identity has acquired a momentum of its own, to which a powerful affect attaches, as is seen in ToPatiliu's hobby of collecting tape-recordings of *tubuan* songs or in the behaviour of those who cling tenaciously to *tambu* saying 'without *tambu* we would not be Tolai; we would be another people'. The same issues of social change, cultural erosion, and choice of identity are raised here that were touched on at the end of my discussion of the Copperbelt material. It will be seen that they lie at the heart of the question of Jewish identity in the United States too. At this point, therefore, let me turn to my final ethnographic example.

\* \* \*

## Aspects of Jewish identity in the United States

'People who have been living in a Ghetto for a couple of centuries are not able to step outside merely because the gates are thrown down, nor to efface the brands on their souls by putting off the yellow badges. The isolation imposed from without will have come to seem the law of their being. But a minority will pass, by units, into the larger, freer, stranger life amid the execrations for an ever-dwindling majority. For better or for worse, or both, the Ghetto will be gradually abandoned, till at last it becomes only a swarming place for the poor and the ignorant, huddling together for social warmth. Such people are their own Ghetto gates; when they migrate they carry them across the seas to lands where they are not.'

Israel Zangwill: *Children of the Ghetto* (1895:x)

Wherever the movement of people occurs, whether it takes the form of internal migration from the rural areas to the city, or from 'tribal' reserve to industrial centre, or of emigration from the homeland to seek a new life in another country, the first, and perhaps continuing, problem is economic survival in the new environment. Successful adaptation to this strange milieu depends on many circumstances: the character of the migration, the skills, technical and social, that the immigrants bring with them, their social cohesion, aspirations, and values; but it depends no less on conditions in the place to which they move, in particular the structure of opportunities that they find there. In some parts of contemporary Africa certain groups have been well-equipped to carve out a favourable and distinctive niche for themselves. Such, for example, are the Hausa of Northern Nigeria who, settling in such cities as Ibadan, have come to play a dominant role in the cattle and kola nut trades (see Cohen 1969). In other parts of Africa, however, as we have seen on the Copperbelt, Africans who were attracted to the towns were predominantly obliged to fulfil the requirement for unskilled manual labour. We have seen too in New Guinea how the position of the Tolai within the wider society is very much bound up with the distinctive role they have come to play not just in the rural, but no less importantly in the urban, sector of the economy. Likewise, in considering the situation of the Jews in America, we find that the kind of niche they were able to secure within the economy has been crucial in their adaptation to their new environment. However, the process by which this was achieved is a much more complex one than in the other cases just mentioned. Jews first came to America more than 300 years ago: they have come at different points of time, from different countries, and with different cultural backgrounds, and on their arrival they encountered at each point vastly different sets of social and economic conditions prevailing in the host society.

The first Jewish colonial settlers were Sephardim, mainly of a wealthy merchant class, with strong links, both family and commercial, with communities in England, the West Indies, or Central Europe. Numbering no more than 2,500 by 1790, and clearly recognizable as a 'middle-class' group, they gathered mainly in a few of the main centres of settlement. Many intermarried and became converts to Christianity, particularly those who settled singly in villages or on the frontier. Yet what is of interest is that this tiny minority did not die out, but formed a series of communities that in some cases have lasted to the present.[36]

It was not until after 1836 that there was a marked rise in the Jewish population when there began the first major wave of mass immigration to the United States. The new immigrants, often arriving as whole families or groups of families from a single locality or country, differed from the already established Jewish colonists in many significant respects. Most of them came from the German states or parts of Central Europe under German cultural influence, where they tended to be artisans and petty traders scattered through the towns with no great concentration in the cities. Unlike the earlier Sephardim, the first Ashkenazi Jews arrived without important business connections; they were generally very poor and financially incapable of entering into wholesale trade. However, taking advantage of the expanding frontier, they followed the routes of expansion. Leaving behind the seaboard cities, they quickly struck inland. Initially, they worked as pedlars, serving a vital function in bringing goods and news to the scattered and isolated homesteads of the frontier. Gradually, as local communities began to take root they opened the first clothing, drygoods, and general stores. Most of the Jewish communities of America were established by these small groups of German Jewish pedlars (Glazer 1972).

By 1880 the total Jewish population numbered about 250,000 of whom the vast majority were of German origin. A remarkable feature of their response to American conditions was the rapidity of their rise into the middle class, a development matched by their increasing integration into the wider society. Founders of fortunes in the burgeoning cities of the Mid-West, they also began to emerge as prosperous merchants and shopkeepers in the South and Far

West. In the East, a hierarchy of German Jewish society grew up, headed by a few wealthy families in banking and merchandising, and comprising a large and prosperous middle class which included many lawyers, doctors, and persons in public and intellectual occupations. Though it is not to be wholly explained in these terms, the adoption of Reform Judaism accurately reflected their new social status and aspirations. The Reform Movement, which had its origins in Germany in the mid-nineteenth century, and was carried across the Atlantic by German rabbis, aimed at developing a form of Judaism more attuned to a modern rationalistic philosophy. This involved stripping Judaism of many of its traditional and most hallowed trappings. In particular, it introduced drastic changes into the order and character of the service of the synagogue, now to be known as temples; but Reform also expressed a central social message, most aptly conveyed perhaps in a comment of Rabbi Isaac M. Wise: 'For our own part, we are Israelites in the Synagogue, and Americans everywhere' (cited in Blau 1965:67). Within a short space of time Reform Judaism had become the prevailing pattern in American Jewish life.

The whole picture was to be radically changed when, from 1881 onwards, there began a new series of waves of immigration on a scale hitherto unimagined. Between 1881 and 1924, when national quotas were introduced and mass immigration came to an end, more than two million Jews entered the country. They came from the countries of Eastern Europe, especially Russia, where, segregated from the wider community and subjected to all manner of restrictions, they had developed over the centuries a distinctive form of Jewish culture — the culture of the *shtetl* (see, e.g. Zborowski and Herzog 1952). Unlike the Slavs and Italians, who were also entering the country in large numbers during this period, the Jews did not come so much in response to the call of industrial opportunity; they came rather to escape conditions which were becoming increasingly intolerable in the homeland (Stein 1965: 160). They arrived for the most part penniless, with meagre possessions, and few skills. They arrived, moreover, at a time when the great westward expansion within America was coming to an end, and where the major economic thrust for the future was to lie in the cities. So, instead of spreading out as the German Jews had done, the Eastern Europeans tended to concentrate in the cities of the East, where jobs were available, particularly in the rapidly developing garment industry. In the congested ghettos of these areas of first settlement, they introduced a new strand into the fabric of American society: a Jewish working class. If for no other reason than sheer weight of numbers, the new immigrants completely transformed the face of American Jewry. Such has been their dominance that some authorities nowadays speak as though internal differentiation within the Jewish community in terms of descent or country of origin has completely disappeared. While it would be a simple matter to show that such a view is not entirely justified, and indeed misses much of the complexity and diversity of modern Jewish life in America, it does embrace the valid point that any contemporary study of Jewish ethnicity must necessarily focus on the Eastern Europeans and their descendants.

Throughout the centuries of the diaspora the basic social institution of European Jewry was the *Kehilla*, a form of social organization that was at once local community and congregation (see Katz 1961; Wirth 1928). Enjoying autonomous status within the framework laid down by specific state or imperial decrees, the internal affairs of the community were administered by traditional Jewish law. Under the governance of this law, the community officers, lay and rabinical, superintended all the affairs of Jewish life. Such a system could not readily be transplanted to the more open conditions of American society, where instead it was the synagogue that developed as the central institution of social life (see Blau 1965). Whereas in Europe the synagogue was only one agency of the Jewish community, in America it became *the* community. And this was true not only of the most recent immigrants from Eastern Europe, but also of their predecessors, the first Sephardic colonials and the later German settlers. What chiefly distinguished the latest arrivals from their forerunners, and the role of the synagogue in their lives, was the intensity of their attachment to orthodox observance. Traditional Judaism is what one may term a pervasive religion in the sense that the conduct of the individual is governed by law down to its very minutiae; no detail is too insignificant to escape the universal principle of sanctification, the ubiquitous presence of the Holy. In their observance of these prescriptions (*mitzvot*), the Eastern European Jews were marked by their piety or *frumkeit*. More than this, as Glazer (1972:62) observes, among them were thousands with a fabulous knowledge of traditional law and usage. 'Their congregations had no need for rabbis, let alone "ministers";

even the most ignorant knew the Hebrew text of the prayers and the melodies that traditionally accompanied them, and the whole congregation formed a spontaneous if discordant choir.'

Israel Zangwill's (1895:xi-xii) portrait, though drawing on his knowledge of London's Whitechapel, conveys no less accurately the atmosphere of the synagogues of New York's East Side.

'Decorum was not a feature of synagogue worship in those days, nor was the Almighty yet conceived as the holder of formal receptions once a week. Worshippers did not pray with halted breath, as if afraid that the deity would overhear them. They were at ease in Zion ... They passed the snuff-boxes and remarks about the weather. Prayers were shouted rapidly by the congregation, and elaborately sung by the *Chazan* ... He was the only musical instrument permitted, and on him devolved the whole onus of making the service attractive. He succeeded. He was helped by the sociability of the gathering — for the Synagogue was virtually a Social Club, the focus of the sectarian life.'

However, this general picture needs to be qualified in at least two important respects. In the first place, not all of the immigrants shared the same attachment to orthodoxy. Many had abandoned their ancestral faith even prior to departure from the homeland, and had turned to more secular ideologies. Apart, therefore, from the synagogues, a myriad of organizations rapidly sprang up in the areas of first settlement in which the members could pursue their avid interests in socialism or Zionism, both movements themselves fragmented into many splinter groups. Secondly, exposure to America quickly generated, or more accurately, perhaps, served to speed up,[37] a process of decline in traditional observance. The distinguished American journalist Lincoln Steffens (cited in Rogow 1961:291) recounts how as a young reporter, instructed to follow up word of a suicide, he would pass a synagogue where a score or more of boys were sitting hatless in their old clothes, smoking cigarettes on the steps outside, while their fathers, all dressed in black, with their high hats, uncut beards, and temple curls, were going inside, tearing their hair and rending their garments. To the sympathetic observer, noting the sharp contrast in the behaviour of fathers and their sons, 'rebels against the law of Moses', it appeared to portend a tragic demise: 'Two, three thousand years of continuous devotion, courage, and suffering for a cause lost in a generation.'[38]

Yet with all the rapidity of acculturation to American ways, the inhabitants of the ghettos still lived essentially within an encapsulated Jewish environment. (Even at work, as in the garment industry, where so many were employed, they were surrounded by their Jewish co-workers, and frequently their employers were Jewish too.) Within the ghetto there was room for all shades of opinion, and the many diverse groups could all find a niche within which to cultivate their particular interests. If some found cause to renounce Judaism, they did not thereby cease to regard themselves as Jews; there were many alternative ways of expressing one's Jewishness — in Zionism, for example, or within the framework of a Yiddish-proletarian culture. To all but the discerning few, therefore, the situation was not seen as posing a problem of Jewish identity. This only began to emerge as an issue as the immigrants, particularly those of the second generation, began to move out of the ghettos to areas of secondary settlement, to the smaller towns and cities, and later to participate in the vast movement to the suburbs. In what follows I shall discuss some of the implications of these developments for Jewish identity, but my main purpose is not so much to trace the process of adaptation in detail as to consider the way the problem has been approached by a number of anthropologists and sociologists who have studied it at first hand.

## The second generation in Yankee City

Yankee City is a pseudonym that conceals the identity of a community in New England with a history that began with the early settlement of the Atlantic Coast. By the time it came to be studied by Lloyd Warner[39] and his associates, between 1930-35, Yankee City had developed into a small industrial centre producing shoes, silverware, and textiles. Industrial growth, beginning around 1840, made the town attractive as a source of employment, particularly for Catholic Irish who found employment in the factories. Although thereafter there was only a slight expansion in the local economy, the city was able to absorb an increasing number of new residents, in part because of the need to compensate for a declining birthrate among the indigenous middle class, in part because of the departure of many of their children seeking to improve their economic status in the larger cities of the East or to take advantge of the new opportunities opening in the West. A consequence of these demographic changes was the increasing ethnic diversity of the population, though the original Yankee stock has maintained its position of dominance at the apex of the local class hierarchy. The interplay of class and ethnicity is made immediately visible in the residential pattern. The various ethnic groups, soon after their arrival in the city, settled in the most accessible, and usually the poorest areas and, as their numbers grew in strength, they remained identified with these areas, often for decades. However, with the passage of time, and the gradual improvement of their economic status, there followed the now familiar process of 'ecological succession'.

In contrasting the differential response of various immigrant groups to economic opportunities in America significance has sometimes been attached to the fact that most came from agricultural communities, whereas the adaptation of the Jews to the new conditions was eased by their urban background (e.g. Warner and Srole 1945:54-5). The argument is hardly convincing. Most of the Eastern European Jews, as we have seen, came from small towns, *shtetls*, or villages that could scarcely be rated as 'urban', and few had anything in their prior experience that qualified them for work in the factories. A more plausible explanation (see Glazer 1965: 41-3) is that they were 'workers' who carried with them the values conducive to middle-class success; unable themselves to emulate the rapid rise up the social scale of the German Jews, they saw to it that their children moved beyond the position of wage worker. But whatever the reasons, the facts themselves are fairly clear. The first Jews arrived in Yankee City around the turn of the century, and were quickly absorbed (together with the Armenians) in the shoe factories. Because of the way Warner and Srole have ordered and presented their data, it is impossible to identify the specific careers on which Jews later embarked. What is clear is that by 1913 they were in occupations associated with the lower-middle class. By 1933 they had a far higher occupational status than any other ethnic group, even considerably higher than that of the Yankee City natives themselves. By this time, moreover, many of the filial generation had begun to leave for higher economic attractions in larger places.

In an open society whose values emphasize personal initiative and achievement, upward occupational mobility is a first prerequisite of advancement within the class structure, but a better job or a more remunerative form of self-employment is not in itself enough to attain that end. To achieve class mobility a rise on the occupational hierarchy has to go hand in hand with the acqusition of a number of other interdependent status-value attributes. In the context of Yankee City these were, first, the building up of wealth in the form of money, essential to acquiring the appropriate material status symbols. The move to a 'better' neighbourhood and the purchase of one's house there were of prime importance in this context. Second, the aspirant to higher class status needed to extend the range of his social relationships. In particular, this meant developing personal links outside the ethnic group, and associating oneself actively in the affairs of the wider community. All of this in turn led to demands for behavioural change, not only in one's public conduct, but even within the privacy of the home. Warner and Srole (p. 89) offer the example of a Jewish family who had just acquired a new maid:

'She used to work for the Rands [a lower-upper class family of Yankee stock]. She told us she much preferred to serve meals in the dining room. We used to serve all the meals in the kitchen, as you know. But because she wanted it, we are now serving all the meals in the dining room. She bawls us out sometimes for the things that we do, but she is really right about it, so we respect her for her pains.'

On these criteria all the ethnic groups represented in Yankee City have improved their class position. Each succeeding generation, moreover, shows an advance on the preceding one. There are, however, important differences as between the different groups in their rate of advance. Most rapid of all has been that of the Jews, whose class distribution is set out in *Table 1*.

Rapid upward mobility is likely to generate hostility among those in an already established position who see themselves threatened by the parvenus. Resistance does in fact occur in Yankee City, and an effective system of sanctions operates to keep in place those who display an over-eagerness to crash the class barriers. Nonetheless, according to our authorities, the ethnics of Yankee City have conspicuously succeeded in 'getting ahead' in the local hierarchy, and finding acceptance on the progressively higher-class levels. To the extent that this is so, class mobility implies an increasing measure of acculturation and integration into the wider society. Since about half the Jewish families of Yankee City now belong to

Table 1 *Class distribution of Jews in Yankee City in 1933 by generation**

|         | LL   | UL   | LM   | UM  | LU | UU |
|---------|------|------|------|-----|----|----|
| P1      | 12.1 | 59.7 | 25.0 | 3.2 | -  | -  |
| P2      | 6.8  | 31.8 | 56.8 | 4.5 | -  | -  |
| P (Total) | 10.7 | 52.3 | 33.2 | 3.5 | -  | -  |
| F1      | 0.0  | 39.5 | 55.4 | 5.1 | -  | -  |

*The first immigrant generation is subdivided: P1 represents those of the parental generation who came to America as mature adults, P2 those who reached America before the age of 18. F1 represents the children of all P, the first filial generation.

(Reprinted from p. 73 of *The Social Systems of American Ethnic Groups* (1945) by W.L. Warner and L. Srole. Published by Yale University Press at New Haven, Connecticut.)

the middle class, what are the consequences of this for Jewish ethnicity? Let us follow here Warner's and Srole's further analysis by focussing on two institutions: the family and the synagogue.

We have already noted some of the changes that can occur in Jewish domestic arrangements. In their discussion of the family Warner and Srole concentrate on two relationships: that of husband and wife, and parent (chiefly the father) and child. Already in the P2 generation the former marked subordination of the wife to her husband has given way to a much more reciprocal relationship. Thus they point out, for example, that the P2 wife becomes the purchasing agent and business manager of the family corporation in which the husband fills a position akin to banker. The change here from traditional practice — if there has been change at all — may not be so great as Warner and Srole assume.[40] What is clear, however, is that P2 Jewish housewives, none of whom were in wage employment, and freed from the drudgery of household chores by the presence of a maid and/or the use of labour-saving household appliances, enjoyed a high degree of leisure which they could devote to social activities or participation in communal affairs. The family was thus no longer an inward-directed unit but looked 'outward to the effective community system'. In this respect it had reached a form approximating that of the modern, urban middle-class American family.

In another regard, however, the family was an arena of conflict, chiefly between parents and their children. Many factors contributed to this situation, but the fundamental source of breach lay in the exposure of the children to alternative forms of behaviour and values through schooling and mixing with other children. One common cause of friction, though by no means the only one, lay in regard to the vexed question of traditional observance within the home.

'On the Jewish Sabbath, which includes Friday evening, it is sacrilege to have any form of entertainment in the home. The children, however, not sharing this sentiment, want the radio played for certain favourite programs. In every Jewish home the issue has arisen, and after persistent nagging and threatening to go elsewhere on the part of the children, all but one capitulated.'

The relations of parents and children are thus marked by smouldering tensions that often erupt in outbursts of mutual exasperation. As the example just cited illustrates, one source of this tension, as well as its outcome, lies in the increasing rejection by the children of the ancient mores, and the seeming inability of the parents to do anything about it. There sets in, that is to say, a process of cultural erosion which moves with gathering momentum and increasing pace as generation is succeeded by generation, a development which, as Warner and Srole see it, heralds in the shorter or the longer term the disappearance of the ethnic group. The paradigm of absorption they present emerges no more clearly than in their discussion of the synagogue.

Where for the other immigrant groups of Yankee City it was the church which became the first formally organized structure for the ethnic community, for the Jews it was the synagogue. The first fourteen families who arrived in the 1890s quickly formed themselves into a congregation. To begin with they met for regular prayer in each other's houses, but in 1907, when the number of families had reached thirty-five, they acquired an old building which was converted into a synagogue. The temper of its founders is perhaps reflected in the comment of one young woman speaking of her father.

'Last Sukkoth [The Feast of Tabernacles] it was raining pitchforks, and since on holidays you cannot carry even a handkerchief, not to speak of an umbrella, my father couldn't go to the *shul* [synagogue] ... It was the first time in years and years that he hadn't been to *shul* on Sukkoth. And he said to me then that he felt his life had ended.'

The pattern of strict observance represented here was to pass quickly. By the time the study of Yankee City was undertaken, regular attendance at the daily and Sabbath services in the synagogue was chiefly confined to the handful of surviving members of the P1 generation. Only on the High Holy days (Rosh Hashona and Yom Kippur) was there a large turn-out, and even then attendance was not universal. Even more striking perhaps is that only twenty-five men 'belonged' to the congregation.[41]

Involved here is something much more fundamental than simple non-attendance of a religious service. Observance of the Sabbath, regarded as the most important day in the Jewish calendar, is central to the total complex of orthodox practice; once Sabbath observance was undermined, the whole edifice itself was threatened with collapse. A number of the P1 generation were content to remain junk pedlars; this did not bring in a large income, but it gave a measure of independence that allowed them to refrain from work on the Sabbath. Others who had gone into business or ran shops were compelled to bow, if reluctantly, to the harsh economic realities of American life: Saturday was the busiest day of the week. In their case, though their behaviour no longer complied with the injunctions of Torah, they still acknowledged the validity of its norms and prescriptions. Among the P2 generation, however, quite a different attitude already prevailed. Quite apart from any question of attendance at synagogue, in the service of which they found many offensive features, they had abandoned *kashrut*, the dietary laws around which a good deal of the organization of the household revolved, and one of the main barriers to freer intercourse with one's Gentile neighbours, friends, and business associates.[42] Some of the womenfolk were evidently afflicted with feelings of guilt by this flouting of the rules, for they found it difficult to admit to outsiders that they no longer kept a kosher home. With the emergence of the filial generation to maturity, even this vestige seemed to have disappeared. For these younger people Judaism had become 'old-fashioned and meaningless', and all the evidence suggested that they had broken completely with the system. To Warner and Srole it appeared that the process of progressive defection of successive generations of Jews from their religious system was nearly completed among the children of the immigrants themselves. Given this disintegration of the religious sub-system, on which so much of what was distinctive in Jewish social life was based, the implications for the survival of the community seemed clear and unambiguous.

Against the backdrop of this analysis, and in the context of the times — it was the height of the Depression — it comes as something of a surprise to learn that towards the end of 1932, during and immediately after the High Holidays, the Jewish community of Yankee City 'suddenly galvanized itself into a burst of organized action'. In a period of a few weeks, through a series of mass meetings, close to $10,000 was raised within the community to purchase outright a building for conversion into a new synagogue. As Warner and Srole themselves acknowledge (p. 206), the episode appeared 'to be incongruous and completely non-logical'; the matter, and no less the enthusiasm it generated throughout all the sections of the community, called for explanation. What was particularly striking was that it was the younger men, some of whom had not attended a service for years, who took the lead in the campaign for the new synagogue. The campaign itself followed the death of a number of the $P1$ generation. The community was thus confronted with 'a crisis of age-grade movement'. The elder $P1$ generation, alone represented in the congregation, served to maintain the synagogue structure and to articulate the community with the extended religious system which is identified with the whole Jewish society. The dying out of this generation thus threatened the extinction of the synagogue structure, and the collapse of the community as a Jewish community, together with the abandonment of its links with other Jewish communities. If it were to survive, then the younger men of the $P2$ generation had to move into the synagogue structure in order to keep it active in the community system. Warner and Srole point out (p. 210) that every man in the younger $P1$ and $P2$ generations joined the congregation, fifty-five of them in one night.

Yet what is of interest is that these events, and the interpretation they gave of them, did not lead Warner and Srole to any questioning of their basic assumptions. While it was clear that the Jewish community of Yankee City was not yet completely moribund, what had happened was in certain regards still in line with the expectations of the paradigm. The new synagogue did not foreshadow a return to orthodoxy, but suggested rather a move in the direction of some modified form of Judaism, more harmonious with its American context, and more in keeping with a middle-class image.

The new synagogue, formerly a church, and offering one of the most beautiful places of worship in the city, was itself a status symbol, a mark of the Jews' increasing integration into the wider society. Concluding their discussion of the role of the ethnic churches, Warner and Srole point out that the P1 North Irish (Protestant) had been directly assimilated by Yankee City. By contrast, the F2 South Irish (Catholic), the longest established immigrant group there, were only now close to assimilation. The assumption, left unstated in this context, was that the Jews would not be very far behind (see p. 290). For the anthropologists, as for some of their older informants saddened by the manifest decay of religious orthodoxy, there appeared to be no future for the Jews as a distinctive group within the wider American society.

## From gilded ghetto to the suburbs

When Warner and Srole conducted their study of Yankee City, the younger men of the P2 generation, as we have just seen, had only recently moved into positions of leadership within the community. How the filial generation, in its turn, would stand up to this test still lay in the future; as for the third generation, most were still very young and few, if any, had yet reached marriageable age. The study of North City, carried out by Kramer and Leventman (1961) in 1957, is valuable therefore in helping to provide a more rounded picture of the adaptation of the second generation, as well as a glimpse of the emerging world of the third generation.

Like Warner and Srole, Kramer and Leventman focus on the interplay of generation and class and the bearing these have on ethnicity. In general the processes they discover at work are similar, but since their observations were of different phases in the unfolding of a continuing process, the two studies differ in their emphases: whereas the issue that chiefly attracted the attention of the anthropologists in Yankee City was class mobility, Kramer and Leventman were more interested in the internal differentiation of North City's Jewish community. Such differentiation they found conveniently expressed in the distinction between clubniks and lodgniks: the wealthier members of the community who had settled in the more attractive neighbourhoods on the south side of the city who belonged to the Pinecrest Country Club, and those who were less prosperous, had stayed on the north side, closer to the area of first settlement, and belonged to the Silverman Lodge of B'nai B'rith. Among the clubniks there were some of German descent, but both groups were of predominantly Eastern European stock. They were marked, however, by quite distinctive life-styles. Clubniks, for example, were affiliated to the Reform Temple, lodgniks to the Conservative Synagogue.[43] Associated with this were clear differences in the matter of religious practice. Though observance was scarcely high in either group, among lodgniks 78 per cent attended High Holiday services compared to 48 per cent among the clubniks. Again, while there was no member of the Lodge who could claim to be strictly kosher, 24 per cent observed at least some of these laws; among the clubmen even the most minimal observance had been abandoned.

Such abandonment represents only the negative aspect of the process of differentiation; the more positive lay in the varying degree to which the two groups adopted the practices and values of the wider society. Two minor, though revealing, illustrations are to be found in the changing patterns of naming and in the observance of Christmas. None of the lodgniks had an Anglo-Saxon surname, whereas 28 per cent of the clubniks did. The latter enjoyed particularly high prestige among their fellow Jews and frequent interaction with Gentiles. Though the motives for a change of name may sometimes be complex, one component here, as Kramer and Leventman observed (p. 89), was the desire on the part of 'far-sighted parents' to see their children enjoy the advantages of non-Jewish social circles. There were also important differences between the two groups in regard to the observance of Christmas. Among clubniks 26 per cent displayed Christmas trees and exchanged family gifts as against 4 per cent of lodgniks. Members of both groups sent Christmas cards to non-Jews. More interesting, however, is that more than half the clubniks sent cards to their fellow Jews; lodgniks, by contrast, still committed to a vestige of their religious tradition, confined their Christmas greetings almost entirely to Gentiles.

Internally differentiated by contrasting life-styles, values, and aspirations, what then bound the Jews of North City into a single community? North City in fact was a highly organized community with a range of institutions paralleling those of the wider society, and all affiliated to the Federation for Jewish Social Service which co-ordinated the activities of local social service and fund raising agencies. But in itself this provides no answer to the question, for the Federation was a voluntary agency without the sanctions that characterized the traditional *Kehilla*. Moreover, the maintenance of separate Jewish social services was an expensive matter, the main burden of which fell on the wealthier members of the community. One of the hypotheses which Kramer and Leventman set out to test was that the higher the status in the Jewish community, the greater the acceptance of non-Jewish values and the less the acceptance of traditional Jewish values. In one regard alone was this expectation not upheld: while 86 per cent of clubniks were active in non-Jewish causes (as against 8 per cent of lodgniks), 92 per cent of the clubniks actually contributed most to Jewish philanthropies. Part of the reason for this undoubtedly lies in the exclusion of Jews from full participation in the Gentile community, but the internal pressures were also considerable. The leading members of Pinecrest were wealthy businessmen whose financial success was in many important respects bound up in their ethnic segregation; they were able to turn their marginality to economic advantage, and in-group clubs and associations further served to promote their business interests (Kramer and Leventman pp. 67-9). At one point Kramer and Leventman make passing reference to 'potlatching', and there is indeed much in their account that is reminiscent of the way, for example, 'big men' in Melanesia employ their wealth to acquire status and power within the community. Kramer and Leventman offer no description of the kinship and political systems of the Jewish community of North City, or of its ceremonial life, but what still emerges clearly from their analysis is that while the two strata live differently, their social relations are mutually orientated.

The second generation in North City, then, located in the better neighbourhoods, emulated the structure of the host community with a wide range of institutions parallel to those of the society at large. Yet it retained its fundamentally ethnic character. It was, as Kramer and Leventman remark (p.11), a gilded ghetto whose social life was carried on exclusively with Jews of appropriate status. The institutions were all middle class, but the participants were all Jewish. Dominated by the urge for financial success, its values were predominantly those of the *nouveaux riches*. Now economically secure, though still uncertain of its social status within the wider society, the second generation invested its hopes in its children, grooming them for a life outside 'the pale of the gilded ghetto'.

Education of the children was a favoured form of investment of the second generation. Twenty-nine per cent of the sons had completed a college education, and a further 36 per cent had received graduate or professional training. While many followed their fathers into the family business, those who lacked this opportunity or were unwilling to take advantage of it were equipped to enter the independent and salaried professions. In an expanding economy, marked by the opening up of a range of new occupations, they were able to embark on careers, entry to which, the fact that one was Jewish, presented no barriers, and which carried high status in the Gentile world. This more than compensated for the fact that the young professionals often lacked — as yet — the earning capacity and wealth of their fathers. The latters' attachment to 'material' values earned their disapproval. But they were not averse to wealth; they saw its purpose rather in making possible a more cultivated life-style. Curiously, the pursuit of this end does not appear to have involved a further dilution of their attachment to Judaism. Contrary to the expectations of the Warner and Srole model, no significant differences emerged in the pattern of observance as between the parental and filial generations. Since religious affiliation no longer presented the same obstacles to career advancement, it presented less of an issue. Kramer and Leventman report that the majority took a tolerant, even favourable, attitude towards religion, for it did not now require the rigour of daily devotion nor set them apart from non-Jews. 'The accepted rituals are the ones which most closely approximate the religious practices found in Gentile homes' (p. 160). These attitudes are, indeed, highly appropriate to the life of the suburbs, to which the young professionals have now moved. There, where considerable importance attaches to church attendance, Judaism does not mark one out as 'different from other people'; one merely belongs to a different congregation.

Yet if the life of the suburbs is supportive in some regards of Jewish identity in its religious aspects, it also raises in acute form questions about Jewish ethnic identity. As Kramer and Leventman point out (p. 175), the suburb is a setting so intent on the virtues of sociability that it brooks no strangers.

'No one can be in it, and not of it; participation is the price of suburban residence for Jew and Gentile alike ... No longer protected from his surroundings by the social isolation of the gilded ghetto, the young Jew must respond to the demands of his community, conforming to the expectations of his neighbours as neighbours rather than as Jews. He is drawn into a social situation in which ethnic uniqueness is not recognized as legitimate grounds for differential association.'

In such an environment could ethnic distinctiveness be maintained? It was to this issue that Sklare and Greenblum directly addressed themselves in their study of Lakeville, *Jewish Identity on the Suburban Frontier* (1967), to which I now turn.

North City appears to have been a fairly typical small town of the American Midwest. Though it enjoyed quite a prosperous economy, it lacked the affluence and established wealth, the diversity, and the range of intellectual and cultural activities of the great metropolitan centres of the nation. In these regards the setting for Sklare's and Greenblum's study offers a striking contrast. Lakeville, attracting its residents selectively from among the business and professional elite of Lake City, one of the country's major industrial centres, was among the more exclusive suburbs which began to spring up in the area in the 1920s and experienced a further flowering in the late 1940s. Although it has seen many changes over the years some of the characteristics that marked its beginnings as a summer resort for the elite of Lake City are still very evident. The community now possesses five private golf clubs, as well as a yacht club, and there are a wide range of public and recreational facilities. One of its outstanding features is its Centre for the Performing Arts at which first-class musical and theatrical programmes are presented during the summer season. There are also community concerts during the winter. Although Lakeville's population now includes a significant proportion of working-class families, there is no heavy industry, and relatively little light industry there; most workers are employed in the servicing industry, particularly in retail establishments which are the main form of local business. In a word, Lakeville provides a picturesque setting for a cultivated suburban way of life. Like most of its residents, the Jews of Lakeville are socially middle class or upper class in occupation or income. What then becomes of Jewish identity in this kind of environment?

The picture that Sklare and Greenblum present of the religious life of Lakeville is very similar in its basic features to that of the third generation in North City. Stated briefly, religious practice, measured in terms of the observance of a range of *mitzvot*, traditionally regarded as obligatory, is at a very low level in most of the homes. At the same time the data do not point to a negative exponential curve of the kind implied in the Warner and Srole model. Rather the curve levels out and becomes stabilized at a certain minimal level. Indeed, in certain regards one detects a reversal of hitherto dominant tendency. One of Warner's and Srole's respondents had remarked sadly that in Yankee City 'the Shabbos was dead'. Saturday in Lakeville too is just another day. The Jewish Sabbath, however, begins at sundown the previous evening, and there appears to be increasing observance of this among some younger families, marked by the traditional lighting of the Sabbath candles, the recitation of the *Kiddush* (sanctification), and the sharing of a special Friday night family meal.[44]

The Jewish community of Lakeville is not only wealthier and more established than that of North City, it is also more heterogeneous in its social composition. It includes among its wealthiest and most respected citizens long-settled German families, some of whom are now represented in a fourth generation of mature adults. There are also different strands among the Eastern European Jews who arrived in Lakeville at different times. This diversity is reflected in the five congregations — one Conservative and four Reform — that have been established within the community. Building a synagogue and maintaining it, as well as paying the salary of the Rabbi, is a costly business. We may wonder why the Jews of Lakeville are prepared to accept this self-imposed form of taxation when the typical Jewish resident neither attends services with any regularity nor observes much of the prescribed ritual in his home. Yet the fact is that at any given moment some two-thirds belong to a synagogue or temple, and that more than nine out of ten families whose children are all aged eighteen or over are past or present members. We have seen in our account of North City how considerations of status can be important in this connection, but what emerges more clearly from the Lakeville study is the way in which affiliation to synagogue or temple expresses the explicit concern of parents that their children acquire some knowledge of Jewish religion and of the history and cultural heritage of their people.

Since most parents lack the will, still less the knowledge, to instruct their children themselves, the demand naturally arises for some kind of Jewish schooling.[45] In its minimal form this was provided by the Sunday School. Even here of course we cannot discount the pressure emanating from the wider society and mediated to the parents through their children. Children who did not attend Sunday School, but had Gentile friends who did, might be led to wonder in what way they were different and why they were left out. That the main thrust came from within, however, is to be seen in the account of the founding of Lakeville's first Jewish Congregation, the Isaac Mayer Wise Temple. Already in the pre-World War I period religious classes had been organized for children living in the area known as the Heights. But while parents returned to Lake City from time to time to attend services there, such commuting was not practicable for children being prepared for the rite of confirmation. To the adherents of Classical Reform this ceremony carried great significance, for without it the child was not accepted as being a member in good standing of the Jewish faith. Thus the Temple traces back to the privately organized classes designed to prepare children for confirmation; it emerged from a school and not, as in the case of the synagogue established by the first generation immigrants, whether from Germany or Eastern Europe, out of the need for a *minyan*, a quorum of ten adult males who worshipped together.

The importance of the children for affiliation to a congregation is also seen in the way in which membership of a synagogue is linked to the life cycle. Only 19 per cent of families in which all the children were under school age belonged to a synagogue. However, the affiliation rate tripled to 56 per cent in the early school phase and rose to 87 per cent when there were children in the peak years of religious education. In the later phases of the family life cycle, although there is no stampede from affiliation, there is an overall reduction in membership among families all of whose children are beyond high school age. Although other factors are relevant, it appears then that synagogue affiliation is tied chiefly to the concern of parents to expose their children to Jewish education and to give them a Jewish identity. Such concern of course provides no measure of the intensity of their own religious convictions. On the contrary, in no other regard perhaps do Lakeville Jews reveal so clearly the ambivalence, even the contradictoriness, of their attitudes towards their ancestral faith as in the matter of education. Witness the statement of one parent which, one suspects, would be shared by many others: 'I like Schecter [the Conservative Synagogue]. It gives my boy a good Hebrew education. And they've left me alone — I've never been inside.'

The synagogue thus retains its significance as a symbol of religious continuity. Moreover, the very diversity of the institution in the Lakeside context allows for the incorporation of the largest number of families within the religious structure. Epiphenomenally, however, the synagogue also comes to play a social function which represents perhaps its major contribution to the maintenance of ethnic boundaries.[46] Like the churches, in their efforts to attract and retain membership, the synagogue too has been obliged to develop programmes to cater for a wide variety of secular interests. Even when they belong to a synagogue the Jews of Lakeville do not attend services to anything like the same extent as their Christian neighbours; they are, however, equally, if not more, active where purely social participation is concerned.[47]

Participation in the affairs of a synagogue is a voluntary form of inclusiveness wholly acceptable within the framework of values of the wider Lakeville community. Lakeville might not tolerate ethnic distinctiveness, but it does recognize 'religions'. The Jews of Lakeville are full citizens and play an active part in the public life of the suburb. Yet what is also clear is that the pattern of inclusiveness expressed within the synagogue is also maintained outside it. One interesting feature to which Sklare and Greenblum draw attention is in changes in the pattern of social interaction between the generations: where in the parental generation much of one's social contact was within the 'family' (i.e., with relatives), some 88 per cent of the respondents in the Lakeville study spent more time socializing with friends rather than with relatives. Even more remarkable, given the many opportunities for establishing friendships outside the Jewish community, such ties are 'predominantly — almost overwhelmingly — with other Jews'. Though more acculturated than their parents, and frequently moving in a more mixed environment, respondents made their close friendships with Jews as often as did their parents.

Its stability apart, there are a number of other features of the friendship pattern that merit comment. First, throughout the period of schooling children mix freely and establish many friendships with non-Jews, but as they achieve adulthood and marry they acquire and stabilize a relatively homogeneous pattern of close Jewish friendships. Second, the tendency holds irrespective of degree of observance or synagogue affiliations. Thus an affluent businessman, a member of Einhorn Temple (Classical Reform), who was not given a Jewish upbringing by his parents and claimed ·to be entirely uninterested in religious matters, explained his preference for contact with fellow Jews: 'There are cultural differences; we have common backgrounds, interests, and standards as Jews.' Finally, we may note that of those who reported that their friendship circle included a minority of Gentiles, it turned out in half the cases that the Gentile friend was married to a Jew. Some of those, indeed, identified as Gentiles, were in fact converts to Judaism. As Sklare and Greenblum observe (p. 272), the phenomenon suggests that a certain proportion of intermarried couples have found a place inside the Jewish group, even though the use of the category Gentile in this context also suggests their incomplete 'assimilation'. But incomplete or not, such individuals appear not only to become 'acculturated' to Jewish ways, but also to become detached from Gentile clique groups.

The question of intermarriage can of course become crucial to the maintenance of boundaries between ethnic groups. Since, as we have seen, Lakeville parents are anxious to maintain 'the chain of tradition', it might seem an easy and straightforward task to infer their attitudes to intermarriage. Some, indeed, do express their opposition in plain 'survival' terms. But for many the issue is a more complex one and instead of justifying their stance on the basis of a concern with Jewish identity, Jewish survival, or Jewish religion, they point rather to the difficulties of adjustment, and the likelihood of discord, in a mixed union. As Sklare and Greenblum point out (p. 313), this kind of response neatly expresses the nature of their dilemma as well as suggesting a way out of it. Anxious to see their children marry within the faith, they are no less keen that their conduct be consistent with the liberal views they hold on intergroup relations. Furthermore, they are also seeking to harmonize their desire for Jewish continuity with their acceptance of the individual's right to freedom of marital choice. 'The notion that a Jewish-Gentile marriage is inherently unstable represents a resolution of this conflict; there is freedom to choose, but wisdom dictates that the choice be a fellow Jew.' Sklare and Greenblum might have added that strength of feeling in the matter is also to be gauged by the strenuous efforts that are made, even among the adherents of Classical Reform, to provide favourable settings within which young Jewish couples can meet. One may not be able to control choice, but by manipulating the environment one can at least hope to restrict the range of choice. Contradiction or not, Jewish parents in Lakeville remain effectively committed to the assumption that the group should survive.

The three studies on which I have focussed are of different communities, undertaken at very different points of time. They differ too in their aims and scope, and to some extent in sophistication and scholarship. Nevertheless, they are also marked by a striking similarity of approach based on certain shared assumptions. Thus all adopt a common view of ethnicity which is seen essentially in the terms of Warner and Srole (1945:28) as involving membership in a group with a distinctive culture, and participation in that group. Hence, although ethnic identity is an implicit or explicit concern of all three studies, it is acculturation and/or assimilation which provides the major analytical concepts. I shall say a little more on this elsewhere. For the moment I simply wish to note that this kind of approach leaves unanswered many of the questions that we wish to ask about ethnic identity. Where the interview schedules focus primarily on particular aspects of behaviour, as for example on religious observance, and where the various attitudes expressed are presented not with reference to a particular respondent but to the different topics in which the investigator is interested, we gain little knowledge of the respondent's view of self, with what choices he sees himself confronted, or to what extent, and how, the crisis of ethnicity is experienced.[48] There is, moreover, a second, and rather different, kind of issue. All three studies are of highly organized local communities. To move into a suburb such as West Parricus in North City or Lakeville, and to become affiliated to one of the synagogues or temples, is already to evince some degree of commitment to one's Jewish identity and a willingness to acknowledge, at least to some extent, the sanctions of the community. (The situation may also operate in reverse; that is, it is in response to such sanctions that one joins a synagogue.) But in an open society which encourages a high rate of social and spatial mobility there is no reason why a

Jew, after leaving the parental home, need associate himself with any community. And, indeed, there are many such unattached and unaffiliated Jews. I would argue that for a deeper understanding of ethnic identity, a study of such 'lost' Jews is as crucial as one of those who have remained within the fold. For obvious reasons such studies are likely to be very difficult to undertake and, to my knowledge, there are none available that meet my particular requirements. In the past anthropologists have sometimes made use of the 'life-history' as a useful perspective from which to approach an exotic culture. I suggest that the use of autobiographic texts has also much to offer the anthropologist concerned with more complex situations, not so much because the subjects of such texts are in some sense representative figures, but because they expose to our gaze processes that can too easily elude the sociologist's probes. In the next section, therefore, I have chosen to follow a man, a professing 'non-Jewish Jew',[49] Paul Jacobs, as he wrestles with the question *Is Curly Jewish?* In this book Jacobs (1965) presents a political self-portrait tracing his career as a Trotskyist radical, a trade union organizer, and eventually a writer, but it is also the account of a painful voyage of self-discovery, at the core of which lies the question of his identity as a Jew.

## A 'non-Jewish Jew'?

I have mentioned earlier how among the first Eastern European Jewish immigrants there were many who had already cast off the orthodoxy of the *shtetl*, and who in America expressed their Jewishness by participating in the Yiddish-speaking labour movement. Paul Jacobs came to socialism by a very different route, just as his home background was also very different. His parents, of middle-class mercantile stock, had come to America from Germany some time before the First World War and, able to rely on already established connections, their transition was accomplished without undue disruption. By the time Paul was born in 1918, his father was running a prosperous import-and-export business, and the family was comfortably settled in an apartment house in the upper-Bronx district of New York.

The Jacobs belonged to a Reform Temple, which gave adequate expression to their rather tepid attachment to Judaism. Indeed, as Paul recalls it, the atmosphere at home was as much German as

Jewish; there was no observance of the dietary laws and Christmas was a more important festival than Chanukah. Friday night, the eve of the Sabbath, was marked not by the lighting of candles, but more often was the occasion for a game of bridge with friends. Even so, their Jewish identification remained sufficiently strong for Paul to be sent to Sunday School in order to be prépared for his confirmation. Classes were a bore; by the time he was due to leave Sunday School Paul was already displaying all the familiar signs of adolescent revolt. Assigned as a topic for his graduation address the seventh commandment, he prepared an attack on traditional notions of morality which finished up by suggesting that no Jewish girl should come to the marriage bed a virgin. But whereas the adolescent sons of the Eastern European immigrants might rebel against the 'meaningless' demands that orthodoxy made of them, Paul's early rejection of Judaism had to rest on different grounds. If services at the Temple had to be cancelled during the summer months, it seemed to him that being a Jew was not nearly as important as his parents had said. What repelled him was that the Judaism he was asked to accept was an empty form, lacking in content. Apart from the 'pallid diet of pap' that he was fed at the Sunday School, the chief lesson he appeared to learn at home was a set of defensive standards. Proper behaviour was based on the fear of how the Gentile world might react. A Jew did not make 'trouble'.

Paul appears to have had a close attachment to his mother, whom he describes as gentle. His father, however, was stern and as in later adolescence Paul began to move increasingly in radical circles, their relations became ever more tense and acrimonious. From the parents' point of view there was deep concern with Paul's failure to live up to the standards of a 'good Jewish son'. On Paul's side there was his contempt for, and impatience with, business and the making of money, pursuits which he identified with his parents; but what seemed to goad him no less to fury was their own uneasy identification of themselves as somehow being Jewish, and the argument constantly invoked was that he ought to give up radicalism if for no other reason than that it was bad for the Jews.

Jacob's home background, his schooling at City College, New York — a noted forcing-ground for Jewish intellectuals — where fierce and continuing political debate was a major activity, the fact that he was entering on his young manhood at the height of the Depression, all help to explain his attraction to radicalism. But

Jacobs is too self-aware, and too honest, to imagine that his behaviour was governed by purely conscious processes. He suspects, for example, that one of the unconscious pressures that led him into the radical movement was that it provided an atmosphere in which he could escape being Jewish without any feeling of guilt, as when for a time he adopted the party name Jackson. There was, too, he recognized, the personal need for approbation and recognition which, in complex combination with strong feelings of social indignation, provided the basis for his willingness to accept the discipline and heavy personal demands on which the movement insisted. Both these insights, one supposes, came very much later; as he entered his twenties Jacobs was already a dedicated Trotskyist who had learned that being a radical was not just a matter of endless arguments in cafés or the singing of revolutionary songs at the end of a party meeting.

The Depression had directly affected the Jacobs's household. The father's business failed, and he was forced into struggling for a livelihood as a salesman. Some of the grim realities of the thirties intruded on their world in other ways. With the rise of Nazism in Germany, the Jacobs began to receive pleas from relatives there for assistance in getting out. Yet these events did not lead to any healing of relations between Jacobs and his family; if anything, he became more estranged. What infuriated him was the inability of his parents and their circle to connect what was happening to the Jews in Europe to any wider pattern of developments. For them Hitler's treatment of the Jews — ever 'good Germans' — was incomprehensible, a temporary aberration that would quickly pass. Jacobs's own reactions to the situation were quite different. His opposition to Nazism was rooted, not in the plight of the Jews as such, but in the smashing of the Social-Democrats, the Communists, and the trade unions. His conception of himself was thus in no way altered by these events. He was not stimulated to any greater interest in Jewish matters, nor did he evince much interest in the newspaper reports of the day, of the tensions that were building up between Arab and Jew in Palestine. Because the coming World War, which now appeared inevitable, was to be an imperialist war 'we put out of our minds the particular horror to which the German Jews were being subjected, trying not to let the fact that we too were Jews influence our judgment about what we believed to be the only way Nazism could be defeated'.

Against this background, it comes as something of a surprise to find Jacobs embarking after the war on a new career as a 'professional Jew'. The move, however, implied no change of heart or commitment. Discharged from the army, he had experienced dismal failure in trying to establish a labour weekly; he had returned to the long familiar and always depressing hunt for a job when, through an old contact, he was offered a post in the labour relations section of the American Jewish Committee. Even then he felt rather dubious about working for a Jewish organization. However, he quickly lost whatever embarrassment he felt about 'suddenly becoming Jewish', when he discovered that being a 'professional Jew' made little difference to his personal life beyond the fact that in addition to the standard holidays he could now enjoy the Jewish ones too. Moreover, the emphasis of the Committee's work, particularly where it concerned the non-Jewish world, was not heavily Jewish. Such an arrangement suited Jacobs perfectly; it provided him with a base from which he could fight prejudice and discrimination without any need to be Jewish. 'It was the organizational expression of my own ambivalence about being Jewish, my own unclear wish to be something other than what I was.' And, indeed, most of his work was unconnected with Jews, for he was dealing chiefly with labour unions over the issue of discrimination against Blacks.

Later, when he and his wife decided to move to California, his work for the American Jewish Committee involved him much more closely in communal affairs, for in Los Angeles he was required to serve as an ex-officio member of the Jewish Community Council. 'Communist infiltration' was a lively issue in California in the late forties, of which even the otherwise sedate Community Council was obliged to take notice. As a former Trotskyist — he was no longer affiliated to any group — Jacobs, long familiar with Communist tactics and politically more sophisticated than many of his colleagues, found himself at the centre of a number of ugly political tussles. Such episodes, however, were peripheral and he soon became bored with the non-ideological professional Jewish atmosphere, as well as the routine of office work; he hankered for the action and sense of purpose he had earlier found as a union organizer in Rochester. Shortly afterward he left the AJC to take a job as union representative for the Oil Workers' International Union. One of the attractions of the job lay in getting away from the role of 'professional Jew'; but it also offered the opportunity to get away from the role customarily taken by Jews in American unions — apart from the needle trades and social work, which had large numbers of Jews among the rank and file membership, as well as in the leadership, they tended to be found mainly in research, legal, education, or editorial jobs. In view of this it is rather curious that he should have continued his membership of the Community Relations Committee of the Jewish Community Council. Aware of this himself, he attributed it to a mixture of guilt and a liking for the status it gave him.

To this point then we have an impression of a man whose identity, at least in its ethnic aspects, was built up around what psychoanalysts refer to as the mechanism of denial. This is not to say that Jacobs refused to acknowledge his Jewish origins. On occasion, indeed, as when confronted with some stereotyped expression of anti-semitism among his union members, he would draw their attention to the fact that he himself was Jewish. It is rather that in his own conception of self the issue was without significance and had no bearing on the choices he made touching the conduct of his life. Yet, as we have just seen, there are also hints of change in his position. But because identity is a continuing quest which proceeds, like the process of physical growth itself, through-out life, because, moreover, it proceeds at the unconscious as well as the conscious level, there is no easy way of establishing the points at which a decisive switch has been made. There are cases no doubt where change in the image of self is dramatically sudden, but usually it involves a more gradual and cumulative assimilation of a variety of experiences. So it appears to have been in Jacobs's case. There was, for example, the case against the International Labor Workers' Union which ended in its expulsion from the Congress of Industrial Organizations. It was a painful experience for Jacobs, particularly when the leader of the ILWU, Harry Bridges, an Australian Communist and an almost legendary figure on the West Coast, forced one of the witnesses introduced against him to reveal that he had changed his name from Morris Stein to M. Hedley Stone. In this 'stripping' of the witness of his name, worn like a piece of 'clothing, covering his Jewishness from the sight of the world', Jacobs experienced a sense of his own 'nakedness'. Then there was the spy-trial of the Rosenbergs which touched not only Jacobs's own sensitivities, but appears to have generated widespread agitation among American Jews.[50] For Jacobs the case raised 'all sorts of ugly questions'. Some concerned the conduct of the trial, some its outcome, but some were also personal. 'Why should I', he asks, 'the emancipated Jewish union official, have cringed every time one of the Rosenbergs made a reference to their being Jewish — used being Jewish, so to speak, as a device to explain what they were?' Not very long afterwards he was dismissed from his job with the Oil Workers' Union. Unanticipated, it gave him a sharp jolt. 'For confrontation with self', he remarks, 'I can recommend getting fired.'

> 'The shock forced me to shake off some of my fantasies about myself and accept some of the realities. I wasn't going to be president of the Oil Workers' Union, and to some extent at least I wasn't going to escape being Jewish. I continued to joke about my Jewishness, but slowly a different way of coping with this element of myself was opening up for me.' (Jacobs 1965: 208, 209)

It is perhaps in his attitude towards the State of Israel that his changing concept of self, as well as his continuing dilemmas, are most clearly revealed. Given his past, his response to the establishment of the State in 1948 was wholly consistent with his ideological stance. More personally, the idea of a Jewish 'homeland' was one to which he was opposed, for it implied that he was not at home in America. That was an unacceptable concept, even in his unconscious, where 'being Jewish had little importance to whatever I imagined myself to be'. Some years later, however, he was brought into contact with an Israeli called Evron, an official of the Histadrut, on a liaison assignment in America. The two men quickly became friends. A number of features impressed Jacobs about the Israeli: he made no 'hard sell' for Israel; unlike so many of the American Zionists of Jacobs's acquaintance, who could bring no sense of reality to the issue, Evron could discuss the limitations and liabilities of his country as freely and honestly as could Jacobs those of America. No less striking was his seeming freedom from those conflicts about what being Jewish meant which plagued Jacobs: 'whatever fantasies he had of himself, he must have been Jewish in all of them.'

A second friendship with an Israeli, this time an artist living at Big Sur, confirmed the impression. Some time later he paid his first visit to the country. Other visits followed, including one when he was able to get himself an assignment to report the Eichmann trial. An incident at Lod airport conveys something of the country's impact upon him. He had gone out to welcome his wife. One of the first passengers through customs and passport control was a rabbi. The rabbi was immediately surrounded by his disciples, kissing his coat and seeking his blessing. Then they started dancing around him, singing at the top of their lungs, their heads flying. Jacobs comments: 'As I watched, I realized that if I had been a witness to this same scene at an airport in the United States, I would have been embarrassed. Here I was not, for there were no Gentiles to witness behaviour I would have thought of as unseemly.'

There were other more positive reasons why Jacobs quickly felt at home in Israel. There were reunions with friends, the Israelis whom he had met at home as well as old comrades from the days of the 'movement' who had since settled in the country. Above all there was the intense Israeli preoccupation with ideology,[51] and the continuous and animated discussion to which it gave rise. The milieu was both stimulating and familiar, reminiscent of the political atmosphere in which he had spent much of his own young manhood. 'I found myself very much at home in Israel, not so much because it was a Jewish country but because it was a semisocialist Jewish one.'

Yet the visit to Israel was also in important respects a highly disturbing experience. There were, of course, as one would expect, features of Israeli society which he found objectionable, such as the powerful position of the orthodox rabbinate. But such matters were not the main source of his unease. It was Israel itself, the fact of its existence, by which he felt threatened, for it threw into question a whole set of assumptions around which he had built his life. What sets Israel apart, he says, is that it is a Jewish state. How then is it possible to separate synagogue and state as is done elsewhere in the modern world? What would be Jewish about Israel then?

The problems of Jewish identity in the State of Israel have been pondered by other writers (see, e.g. Leslie 1971). In Jacobs's case, however, behind the posing of his questions one detects a more personal concern, a projection perhaps of his own continuing conflicts. I have suggested earlier that ethnic identity is the product of the interaction of external and internal perceptions and pressures. Although he had never attached much significance to anti-semitism as a force in American social life, the Eichmann trial led him to some troubled reflections on American society's acceptance of the Jew.

Returning home, he published an article on the trial which he ended by saying he had always believed 'I was an American who was also, incidentally, Jewish. Now I have started to wonder if the American Gentile world has always regarded me as a Jew who is also, incidentally, an American.' Many of his Gentile friends wrote to reassure him and to point out that he was quite wrong. 'But I didn't really believe all this nice talk from my friends.' It was of course such a perception of the Gentile world, and the assimilation of certain of its values by his parents, that had played so important a part in his own upbringing. 'Don't behave like a kike' (the category term of abuse for a Jew; in this context particularly an Eastern European Jew) was the constant admonishment of his father throughout childhood, and, like the injunction not to make *'rishis'* (trouble), expresses the essentially negative standards of Jewish behaviour held up to him. A child eager for approbation, he found little Jewish in his environment to bolster a sense of self-esteem. In his early rejection of Judaism, he had rebelled against his parents, but he had also absorbed their values more deeply perhaps than he realized. *Is Curly Jewish?* is the story of a man wrestling to rid himself of a negative identity, but with little on which to build a more positive one. In the end the struggle is still unresolved: 'Not quite a Jew seems to be where I am. Not quite a radical, not quite a Jew.'

\* \* \*

## Ethnicity and identity

My discussion so far has been built up around the presentation of three 'ethnographic' profiles. The profiles reveal a number of situations which vary considerably in their internal structure. There are differences too in the way in which I have presented them, each being drawn from a different perspective and emphasizing rather different features. Thus in handling the Copperbelt material I was chiefly concerned with relations between 'tribal' categories, in New Guinea I examined a changing situation mainly from the vantage point of a particular group, while in the case of the American Jews the perspective has been predominantly an intra-group one. In the first two instances my approach has been influenced by the conditions and setting in which I carried out my fieldwork, and of course by the fact that I have been able to make use of my own observations; in the third case I have had to work within the constraints set by the literature on which I chose to focus. My central concern throughout, however, has not been to highlight the differences between the three situations, but to present them as variations around a theme, varying expressions of ethnicity and identity, amenable to analysis in terms of the same body of concepts and ideas. At this point, therefore, it becomes necessary to subject my use of the terms ethnicity and identity to rather more careful scrutiny.

The expression ethnicity appears to have crept into the literature only quite recently and, as Glazer and Moynihan (1974:33) have remarked, 'one senses a term still on the move'. It derives of course from the earlier use of the concept of ethnic group; we are thus able to identify, at least retrospectively, a number of theoretical positions that anthropologists and sociologists have adopted in regard to ethnicity. Until quite recently the prevailing view among American social scientists was that ethnic groups were to be regarded as cultural groups. This was the view that informed Warner's and Srole's approach to the study of ethnic groups in Yankee City, and although later scholars were to carry further and refine the techniques and methods of enquiry initiated by Warner and his associates, their underlying assumptions continued to exert a strong influence on the growing number of empirical studies being conducted throughout America. Given a definition of ethnic groups as cultural groups, it followed almost inevitably that a concept like assimilation should develop as the central tool of analysis in the understanding of ethnic change. Some of the logical or methodological objections to which this approach lays itself open have been cogently stated by Barth (1969). Here, therefore, I need only add how a preoccupation with 'custom' or 'culture' leads to a blindness to social structural factors. A good example of this is to be found in Warner's and Srole's (1945:283) claim that because both immigrant and host society knew the so-called 'old American' culture was itself new and ultimately 'immigrant', this feeling created a 'certain toleration in the attitude of the host society'. In the face of such statements it is difficult to resist the conclusion that analysis and ideology had become deeply interpenetrated, yielding the expectation that the cultural features which distinguished one ethnic group from another would inevitably lose their strength in a modern or modernizing society, and that there would be an increasing emphasis on achievement as against ascription in the definition of social status. Given, too, the impact of education and communication through the mass media, as well as the arrangements of the national economic and political systems, the rapid demise of ethnic groups as a major principle of social organization seemed inescapable.

It has taken time for the weaknesses of the 'assimilation model' to become apparent. In the end, however, the increasing extent to which social scientists have had to confront 'the persisting facts of ethnicity' has forced a review of methodological premises and a search for new models.

Within America Glazer and Moynihan's study *Beyond the Melting Pot* (1963) represented an important break from earlier approaches when, examining the contemporary status of ethnic groups in New York City, they began to speak of them as interest groups. Seeking to conceptualize his data from West Africa, a similar line of approach has been developed by Abner Cohen (1969, 1974b), for whom ethnicity is essentially a political phenomenon, involving a struggle for power among ethnic groups in furtherance and defence of their collective interests. There is no question that we are dealing here with a major dimension of ethnicity, and the competitive element certainly emerges very plainly in the material which I presented earlier in this essay on the Copperbelt and in New Guinea. To this extent, the treatment of ethnic groups as interest groups marks an advance on earlier analyses, but it also presents difficulties of its own. Neither Glazer and Moynihan or Cohen have offered any analysis of the concept of interest group; its meaning is taken to be self-evident. In Cohen's case this may appear to have been justified by the nature of the ethnographic data. In his study of the Hausa of Ibadan, Cohen was concerned with a group of people occupying a particular part of the city, who formed a political and religious unit as subjects of the Hausa chief and, later, as members of the Tijaniyya order. His analysis shows how this form of ethnic organization, developed in Ibadan, enabled the Hausa to gain control of the profitable cattle and kola nut trades, and at the same time to ward off incursions from members of other groups that might threaten this hegemony. Since so many of those resident in, or passing through, the Hausa quarter were linked, in various ways, into the cattle and kola nut business it is not difficult to see how Cohen comes to conceive of the group as being bound by corporate economic and political interests. Yet it may be questioned how far this provides an adequate model for more complex situations where heterogeneity and diversity are among the chief characteristics of the population. In such circumstances the nature of the group interest may not be at all self-evident; indeed, if Charsley (1974:349) is correct in his reading of the situation in Kigumba, the question of interest may be quite problematic, as it also appears to be in certain American rural communities where groups of different national origin have long lived together but lay great stress on maintaining the boundaries that keep them separate from one another (see e.g. Nair 1969). But even where a set of specific interests can be identified, awkward questions still remain. In a polyethnic situation members of an ethnic group are likely to develop a variety of interests, some of which in some contexts may come into conflict. Class provides an obvious example. And while it is true, as Cohen and others have observed, that in the contemporary situation lines of ethnic cleavage frequently coincide with nascent class divisions, the problem remains why, if interest serves as the chief determinant of behaviour, ethnic affiliation should take precedence over the bonds of class, as it frequently does. Then there is the question of how far a group is tied to a temporal definition of its interests. It seems evident that over considerable periods of time the interests of a group may change, yet the group itself persists. Interest thus becomes a variable, and group the constant, immediately suggesting that there must be some prior factor present by reference to which the group must be defined — unless the survival of the group is itself to be regarded as an interest. That would require stretching the concept to the point where it became meaningless for purposes of analysis; it would have become mere tautology. Finally, it seems worth mentioning that built into this view of ethnicity there appears to be an unstated assumption that ethnic behaviour is governed by rational calculation: as Glazer and Moynihan (1974:33) phrase it, it is interest that guides rational men into social action.[52] This is at best a very partial view which, it seems to me, can only be upheld at the expense of ignoring what is often so striking in so much of ethnic behaviour: that it is the expression of a degree of affect all the more powerful because it is rooted in the unconscious.

Glazer and Moynihan's discussion of the Jews of New York seems to me to illustrate well some of the difficulties just mentioned in adopting a definition of ethnicity in terms of group interests; it also appears to me to reveal their own uneasiness in applying it in this context. Thus they note (1963:140-2) that there is no organization in the city that includes all Jews. Nor is there a central religious organization that serves to bind together the various congregations there; in any case most Jews in New York City do not belong to a synagogue or temple, and many are non-religious or even anti-religious. We are dealing with a group, Glazer and Moynihan tell us, that may never act together and that may never feel together, but nevertheless knows that it is one; it is composed of overlapping minorities which together create 'a community with a strong self-consciousness and a definite character'. Discrimination may have been a potent factor in forging such self-consciousness in the past, but, according to Glazer and Moynihan, is no longer to be detected as a significant force anywhere in the United States. The argument for defining ethnic groups as interest groups seems to me to lose much of its force when Glazer and Moynihan go on to conclude, somewhat peevishly, that a good deal of Jewish togetherness is simply frightened and unimaginative, and its only purpose is to maintain separateness. It seems to me rather that it is this sense of separateness that lies at the heart of the matter, and that has to be explained, and not explained away.

In fairness to Glazer and Moynihan it should be said that they appear not to be completely happy with a mono-factor approach to ethnicity, for they also stress from time to time the importance of the affective component in ethnic behaviour. Their dissatisfaction is reflected in their most recent discussion of the question, which seems to indicate some switch of ground from their earlier position. In order to understand why ethnicity has become such a strong basis for group mobilization in modern society, they now say (1974:37), it is necessary

> 'to modify the bald assertion that ethnicity serves as a means of advancing group interests — which it does — by insisting that it is not *only* [original italics] a means of advancing interests. Indeed, one reason that ethnicity has become so effective a means of advancing interests is that it involves more than interests. As Daniel Bell puts it: "Ethnicity has become more salient [than class] because it can combine an interest with an affective tie."'

In a word, to describe an ethnic group as having interests is one thing, to define it in these terms something quite different. To see ethnicity as essentially a political phenomenon, therefore, is to make the same kind of methodological error as those who earlier defined it in terms of culture; it is to confuse an aspect of the phenomenon with the phenomenon itself. The consequence of this is not only that one is likely to misunderstand various aspects of ethnic behaviour, but that one may also be led to exclude from the field of investigation many of the fascinating problems that ethnic behaviour poses.

A very different approach, which seeks to avoid some of these pitfalls, has been adopted by Barth (1969). The point of departure for Barth's analysis is the primary emphasis he lays on ethnic groups as categories of ascription and identification by the actors themselves. Two important implications stem from this perspective. First, it makes no assumptions about the 'content' of ethnicity: ethnic groups provide an organizational vessel that may be given varying amounts and forms of content in different socio-cultural systems. They may be of great relevance to behaviour, but they need not be; they may pervade the whole of social life or they may be relevant only in limited sectors of activity. A wide field is thus opened up for enquiry. Second, the critical focus of investigation from this standpoint becomes the ethnic boundary that defines the group, not the cultural stuff that it encloses. At the heart of Barth's analysis, therefore, lie the concepts of identity and boundaries, though in fact it is on the problem of boundary maintenance that he principally focusses. Moreover, his chief concern was with the more general question of the interaction of ethnic groups in diverse regions of the world in conditions of relative stability, and he addresses himself only marginally to those circumstances where the emergence of ethnicity has been a response to changing social conditions. Entailed in ethnic boundary maintenance, Barth observes, are situations of social contact between persons of different culture, and ethnic groups only persist as significant units, he adds, if they imply marked differences in behaviour. The situations I have been concerned with in this essay are all marked by a high degree of cultural erosion, and therefore raise in acute form the question not only how the boundary-maintaining mechanisms continue to operate, but why the boundaries should be maintained at all. In seeking answers to these questions it seems to me that we need to look more closely at the nature of ethnic identity; we need to ask, that is to say, how the sense of ethnic identity is generated and transmitted, how it persists and how it is transformed or disappears, yielding to other forms of identity. In approaching these issues it may prove instructive to begin by setting the problem in a wider perspective by glancing briefly at the way a new social category, and its associated identity, emerge in a non-ethnic context.

In his book *Death in Life* (1967) Robert Jay Lifton has attempted to penetrate the nature of the experience, and its consequences, of those who were exposed to the dropping of the atomic bomb at Hiroshima. Among the survivors of that holocaust there emerged within Hiroshima's present population a distinctive category known as *hibakusha*. *Hibakusha* are the permanent victims of exposure to atomic radiation, survivors who have continued to suffer, physically and psychically, its lingering after-effects and whose fate has come to be symbolized by the ineradicable keloid, an area of overgrown scar tissue: the stigmata of *hibakushahood* which are marks of 'defect, disease and disgrace'. The term itself is a neologism, with an official definition that immediately expresses social (or public) recognition of the distinction that separates the afflicted from the non-afflicted. What is also clear, however, is that the *hibakusha* himself has a considerable need to maintain this separation from the 'outsider'. Lifton observes that he divides the world into those who are like him — who have been through the entire ordeal — and those who are not. 'The apocalyptic nature of the experience, along with the taint of its resulting identity, create a semi-mystical quality which the uninitiated cannot be expected to grasp.' This sense of exclusiveness in turn 'serves the further psychological function of lending some value to the *hibakusha* status, whatever its taint; and of creating a group posture from which the sense of special need can be expressed, whatever its ambivalence' (p.196).

The 'group posture' finds expression in a variety of ways. Lifton does not discuss the patterns of personal interaction of or among *hibakusha*, but it is plain that relationships are rapidly built up on the basis of what Barth has called 'shared understandings'. Thus one of Lifton's interviewees reports: 'I met a man one time [who] said, "I experienced the atomic bomb" — and from then on the conversation changed. We both understood each other's feelings. Nothing had to be said ...' Welfare programmes have been developed to deal with the special medical, economic, and social problems of *hibakusha*, and *hibakusha* have also organized their own groups to promote their interests by obtaining improved medical treatment and more extensive medical benefits. One such group, under the leadership of a prominent *hibakusha*, has gone even further, thrusting its way into the wider political arena by allying itself with militant forces within the peace movement in protest against nuclear weapons testing.

The problem of *hibakusha* identity, however, is not exhausted by showing how a new ascriptive social category has come into being or how it has developed into an interest group. Were we to leave the matter there, we should have said nothing about the elements that go into the making of that identity; we should have left untouched such questions as what gives the *hibakusha's* perception of himself its distinctive cast, the processes, psychological and sociological, that are at work to produce this result, and the powerful affective forces that feed and serve to maintain it. It is to such issues that Lifton devotes much of his discussion. I cannot hope here to do justice to the richness and depth of his analysis; in any case it is not necessary for present purposes to follow that analysis in detail, and I simply cite for purposes of illustration a number of features which go into the formation of *hibakusha* identity.

One of the responses which Lifton (1969:13) frequently encountered among Hiroshima survivors was the sense of being 'as-if-dead'. He constructs the inner sequence that lies behind this image of self as follows: 'I almost died; I should have died; I did die or at least am not really alive; or if I am alive, it is impure of me to be so, and anything I do which affirms life is also impure and an insult to the dead, who alone are pure.' Lifton suggests that an expression of this sense can be found in the life-style of many *hibakusha*; it is one of marked constriction and self-abnegation, based upon the feeling that any show of vitality is in some way inappropriate for them, not inwardly permissible. *Hibakusha* retain a sense of infinite culpability, even of guilt and responsibility for the catastrophe itself, despite the fact that they were its victims rather than its perpetrators.

Such an 'identity of the dead', if not unique is at least rare.[53] Other elements contributing to the *hibakusha* identity occur more frequently. *Hibakusha*, for example, reveal certain affinities with other victimized groups, and like them, they undergo considerable conflict over how much of their 'victimized' identity to retain. One way of handling conflicts of this kind is through the mechanism of denial; so we may find *hibakusha* attempting to conduct their lives as if they had never known the bomb. Thus some have moved away from Hiroshima and chosen a place to live where they can hide their identity by refusing to possess, or making no use of, their *hibakusha* health cards, and by putting a distance between themselves and other *hibakusha*. In such cases, however, the denial tends to betray itself by the intensity of its reiteration, and even more importantly, by sudden outpourings of anxiety which can no longer be successfully contained — often in the form of terrifying bodily fears which insist on reminding one that one is, after all, a *hibakusha*. Yet another component which contributes in significant measure to *hibakusha* identity is what Lifton calls the suspicion of counterfeit nurturance. This derives from the sense of sharing a special need which is virtually impossible to fulfil, and from the fact that one is perpetually subject to inauthentic 'offerings' from others. The *hibakusha*, that is to say, both craves and resents special attention. Should his craving be denied, he is left with the sense that his unique death encounter is being ignored and he feels abandoned; but should his special needs meet a response, he views the nurturance offered as inauthentic because it appears to confirm his very weakness, humiliation, and death taint; 'he feels "abandoned" to these hated manifestations of *hibakusha* identity'.

In dealing with denial and counterfeit nurturance we are of course concerned with intra-psychic processes, but this is not to say that the features which go to make up the *hibakusha* identity are to be explained simply in endogenous terms. *Hibakusha* identity is an expression of separateness which is the product at every point of the complex interplay of inner psychological needs and external social perceptions and responses. In Erikson's terms, identity is always psychosocial.

The emergence of a *hibakusha* identity was a response to a situation of such unspeakable horror that our vocabulary provides us with no adequate terms to express it that do not at the same time serve to 'detoxify' it. Partly for this reason, partly because it is an identity which those who currently bear it do not wish to see perpetuated down the generations, the *hibakusha* experience cannot provide a general model for psychosocial identity-formation. On the other hand, precisely because of its extraordinary quality, it does offer some illuminating leads in helping to pinpoint the elements that enter into new social identities generated in less traumatic circumstances.

In the first place there is some disturbance of the natural and/or social environment, bringing disruption to some established sets of social relationships. Generally speaking, in an isolated, homogeneous, and relatively autonomous community the question of group identity is usually unproblematic. In such societies, as Margaret Mead (1970:x) puts it, a man was who he was — inalienable, sheltered, and fed within the cocoon of custom until his whole being expressed it. Nor is the issue of great moment in those situations described by Barth and his associates where long-established conventions provide the basis for stable interaction between groups across well-defined ethnic boundaries, although even in these circumstances interesting questions are sometimes raised about identity change. However, the matter becomes acute, and assumes quite a different complexion, when people are thrust, as in a process of migration, into a strange and unfamiliar environment marked by ethnic heterogeneity, by cultural diversity, and by new ranges of choice. Individuals and groups are thus impelled into fresh confrontations with the self, leading to the buttressing of established forms of inclusiveness or to the emergence of new expressions of exlusiveness and separateness.

Ethnicity in these circumstances finds it most visible expression in the appearance of new social categories. In its most immediate sense, that is to say, ethnicity is a matter of classification, the separating out and pulling together of the population into a series of categories defined in terms of 'we' and 'they'. There is a preliminary point of some importance to be noted here if only because it is so obvious that it is apt to be overlooked. Leach (1967:34) refers to it when he observes that because of the way our language is organized and the way we are educated each of us is constantly finding himself in a position of contrast. '*I* identify myself with a collective *we* which is then contrasted with some *other* ... What *we* are, or what the *other* is will depend upon context.' Though the matter is more complex than I believe Leach allows, the essential point for present purposes is that none of us has just a single identity; as members of society each of us carries simultaneously a range of identities just as each of us occupies a number of statuses and plays a variety of roles. There is indeed a close family resemblance between the concept of identity and the twin concepts of status and role, and it may be useful at this stage to note some of their points of difference. To begin with, it is clear that in some instances there is a close overlap between the three concepts: one can speak, for example, of the category of 'worker' in terms of status, role, or identity. What distinguishes these uses is that when we speak of a worker in terms of status and role we do so on the basis of rules and expectations which are socially defined; identity introduces the new dimension of his perception of self. The coincidence I have just noted, however, is not always necessary, and in other instances we recognize that while status and role may be important contributors to identity, they do not themselves constitute an identity. While my status as a father, and the way in which I fulfil this role, may be important to my sense of personal identity, I am unlikely to formulate it simply in terms of fatherhood. This relates to the further point that in speaking of status and role we are concerned with the process by which the person is broken down into a number of constituent social elements; identity, by contrast, is essentially a concept of synthesis. It represents the process by which the person seeks to integrate his various statuses and roles, as well as his diverse experiences, into a coherent image of self. The contemporary sociological significance of ethnic identity is that so often it becomes what has been termed a terminal identity, one that embraces and integrates a whole series of statuses, roles, and lesser identities. Finally, it may be observed that because identity touches the core of the self, it is also likely to be bound by powerful affect; cognitive in one of its aspects, it is also fed by taproots from the unconscious. The more inclusive the identity, therefore, the deeper its unconscious roots and the more potentially profound the charge of affect.

Ethnicity then begins, as Barth observes, with ascriptive social categories; perception lies at the heart of the matter. But how are these perceptions shaped? One possibility is that indicated in the observations of Rabbi Mendel of Kotzk cited as the headpiece of this essay. This, however, Lichtenstein (1963:174) notes, is a type of self-perception common to all mystics; in order to be oneself there must be no other point of reference, such as the social world in which we live. In that world things are ordered differently and the perception of self always implies a relationship of opposition or at least of contrast, as indicated in the passage earlier quoted from Leach. What this implies is that we are who we are by virtue of some common attribute or property we see ourselves as sharing as against those who are perceived not to possess it. The perception, that is to say, stems from within. Yet this view too inadequately represents the complexity of the matter, for what it overlooks is the way perception of the self takes shape in response to the presence and reactions of others. As Paul Schilder (cited in Young 1971:136) phrases it, 'there is no sense in "ego" where there is no "thou"'. In a polyethnic situation what this means is that the sense of ethnic identity is always in some degree a product of the interaction of inner perception and outer response, of forces operating on the individual and group from within, and those impinging on them from without. Some of the implications that stem from this perspective have already been mentioned in the earlier discussion of the Copperbelt material, and others will be taken up later. The point that seems immediately worth making is the way such an approach allows us to envisage varying expressions of ethnic identity as lying on a continuum marked by positive and negative poles. At the positive pole ethnic identity depends more upon inner concepts of exclusiveness, and upon inner strength and resources; at the other extreme the identity rests on no, or only minimal, inner definition, and is essentially imposed from without.

A good example of the latter is the social category known in the United States as *mischlings. Mischlings* are the offspring of marriages between Jew and Gentile who have usually been brought up in neither a Jewish nor a Christian tradition, and where the home environment has laid little emphasis on ethnic origins. In such circumstances it is likely to come as a painful surprise to the *mischling* to discover in later life, whatever his own views in the matter, that the wider American community tends to regard him as part of the Jewish community (see Berman 1968:211). The identity here is one completely imposed from without and bears no relations to the individual's core image of self; like the *hibakusha* the *mischling* is seen to carry a taint, but unlike the *hibakusha*, he enjoys none of the compensations that derive from the latters' sense of exclusiveness, and which provide the basis for a more positive identity. The case of the *mischling* is yet another extreme example, but in fact elements of negative identity are nearly always present where ethnic groups occupy a position of inferior or marginality within a dominance hierarchy. Abundant evidence of this is to be found in colonial situations, but it is no less characteristic, though in varying degree, of minority groups in modern states: it has contributed importantly to the identity of American Blacks,[54] while Paul Jacobs's account of his own quest for identity illustrates the way it can help to shape Jewish self-perception.

Negative identity exists where the image of self rests chiefly on the internalized evaluations of others, and where accordingly much of one's behaviour is prompted by the desire to avoid their anticipated slights or censure. Positive identity, by contrast, is built on self-esteem, a sense of the worthiness of one's own group's ways and values, which is manifested in one's attachment to them. Yet even in the latter case what needs to be stressed is the way in which certain customs or practices which have come to be seen, both within and without the group, as diacritica of that group, so often turn out on closer inspection to reflect the group's relations with the wider society. Jewish experience offers a number of such examples. Thus the American novelist Herbert Gold, once discussing the future of American Jewry, has remarked, 'Chicken soup and Yiddish jokes may tarry awhile, but the history of the Jews from now on will be one with the history of everyone else'. We may leave to one side the substance of this comment; what is of interest here is the assumption, commonly held by Jew and non-Jew alike, that, as Guttmann (1971:10) puts it, the folkways of *Mitteleuropa* or of the Russian *shtetl* are the essentials of Jewishness. I cannot vouch for chicken soup itself, but what is evident is that many of the dietary habits and preferences commonly thought to be distinctive of American Jews, and for many one of the chief ways by which they continue to acknowledge and express their ethnic allegiance, were adopted long ago from their Gentile neighbours in Europe. However, to focus attention simply on these external aspects of behaviour would be to miss a much more fundamental point. There is scope for a study of the part that ethnic tastes in food can play in maintaining the cohesion of the group and of the other social functions these can serve,[55] but strong attachment to 'ethnic' food also suggests a continuing influence stemming from the earlier mother-child bond. This relationship often reveals its own distinctive ethnic overtones. The Jewish mother, for example, has come to serve in modern American folklore and literature as a prototype of oral indulgence and over-protectiveness, but what is not always recognized is how this trait may itself be a response to external factors, developed as an attempt to compensate for the uncertainties and hostilities of the surrounding environment by providing a more intense form of security within the home. In such ways the external world enters into the formation of identity at its very roots.

The *mischling*, having no basis for the formation of a positive *mischling* identity, remains socially isolated; the *hibakusha*, by contrast, were able to put their sense of sharing an exclusive experience to use in governing their social interactions and in forming their own associations. Ethnic identity provides in a similar way a means for organizing social behaviour. Such was the view that led Mitchell and I to see 'tribalism' on the Copperbelt as providing a framework of categorical relationships which governed a good deal of social interaction among Africans there. Cohen (1969:193) has objected to this formulation; 'tribalism' on the Copperbelt, he points out, *is* a live political and economic issue and not just a matter of categorization to help the African migrant to deal with the bewildering complexity of urban society or to regulate for him such 'domestic' affairs as marriage, friendship, burial, and mutual help. One might reply that neither Mitchell nor I ever asserted that 'tribalism' was just a method of categorization, but that is a minor issue. The more basic point, I believe, is that in underplaying the importance of ethnic groups in regulating informal personal relationships one misses the affective roots of ethnicity, the foundations on which other forms of organization and association can be built. To illustrate: the American Jewish communities on which I have focussed in this essay are all highly organized; they have their own communal institutions, and these in turn are often linked in various ways to national and international bodies. None of these bodies, however, has any formal set of sanctions at its disposal; in the last analysis they all depend on the preparedness of people to pay what are in effect self-imposed taxes. Of course powerful informal sanctions do operate here, but this is only to underline the importance of the ethnic boundaries that suburban Jews elect to maintain in their personal lives. I have referred earlier to those various organizations and associations that have come into being to promote and defend Jewish interests, but they have been relative newcomers on the scene; their emergence pre-supposes a sense of identity that grows out of, and is continually reinforced by, intimate contact with one's own kind. The same point holds with perhaps even greater force on the Copperbelt where 'tribes' were held together through overlapping networks of personal relationships, and not by some institutional structure. Even Tribal Elders, it will be recalled, derived such authority as they possessed mainly from the positions they enjoyed at nodal points within 'home-boy' networks. So, when in speaking of competition for positions of leadership within a trade union on the Copperbelt, Cohen remarks that the leader of an ethnic group would do his best to emphasize ethnic distinctiveness and to mobilize power relations within the group to support him, he is somewhat wide of the mark. On the contrary, such was the complexity of the internal politics of the African Mine Workers' Unions that a Bemba Branch Secretary might well 'engineer' the election of a Nyasa as Branch Chairman as a way of strengthening the local branch's, and his own, position against Union headquarters and its President, a fellow Bemba, to whose policies and political creed he was strongly opposed (see Epstein 1964). It seems fairly clear, indeed, that in the polyethnic situation that obtained on the Copperbelt during the fifties it would have been tactically unwise for any Union leader to have canvassed support on ethnic grounds. In the one detailed account I have presented (1958:135-44) of a Union election it is apparent that voters attached more importance to criteria other than the candidates' tribe; but even on those occasions when 'tribalism' did seem to have an important part in the outcome, the result was not produced by the organized drumming up of 'tribal' support, but by the exercise of choice on the part of voters, influenced by the kin and friends who made up their personal networks.

This is not to deny that ethnic groups have a political role or that support for a Union leader of one's own tribe may not bring some future advantage; such a claim would be absurd. My point is rather that political ethnicity presupposes, and grows out of, a particular kind of structuring of the social environment. One major consequence of this is the way in which invisible boundary lines are drawn marking out spheres of personal interaction. Through this process of encapsulation, to adopt Mayer's term, not only is the sense of identity reinforced, but it also gives these personal bonds a powerful affective charge, providing the force for those informal sanctions that the group is able to command. It is because these bonds are so strong that people readily come to perceive that they share interests of an economic or political kind, and leads them to mobilize for political ends. The emergence of interest groups in this way feeds back on and intensifies the sense of ethnic identity.

Among Africans on the Copperbelt the affective aspect of identity becomes immediately visible when friends meet and greet one another with much mutual salutation and boisterous by-play. It underlines too, if less demonstratively, the preference for one's own kind at a beer-drink or when engaging in other informal activities. In such company, an African will explain, he can speak easily in his own language, he can gossip freely, he can dance and sing his 'tribal' songs. Essentially similar responses were offered by respondents in the Lakeville study in explaining why their friendship circles were so predominantly Jewish. Of particular interest, therefore, is the response of one woman among the 7 per cent who did not have a predominantly or all Jewish circle of friends. Completely alienated from Jewish organizations and religious life and with the most tenuous in-group connection, she yet confessed, 'I'm less comfortable with non-Jews because you feel that they think of you as a Jew. Jews don't really think of you as a Jew' (Sklare and Greenblum 1967:289). Such statements are aptly summed up by Paul Jacobs's (1965:330) reference to the deep uncertainty of many American Jews who think that they are still only on a temporary absence from a pogrom. Where the surrounding environment is so perceived as alien and uncertain, if not actively hostile, it is not difficult to see how, whether one is talking of Africans on the Copperbelt, of Tolai living away from the Gazelle Peninsula and scattered throughout the various parts of Papua-New Guinea, or of American Jews in affluent suburbs, clustering with one's fellows makes for relaxation and some sense of security because such relationships assume a degree of mutual trust. Relationships of intimacy are important to well-being in another way, too, for trusted kin and friends provide one with an audience from which one can hope to receive approbation and reassurance as to one's worthiness.

Thus, attachment to kin, involvement in overlapping 'home-boy' networks, and participation in closed friendship circles serve not only to define the boundaries of the group with which one identifies, they also provide an important mechanism of boundary maintenance. Yet if the identity is to be successfully transmitted, and the boundaries maintained over time, other mechanisms need to be brought into play. Marriage can become a matter of crucial import in this context, since a mixed union may mean not only the defection of a member of the group, but also loss of the children. Cohen (1969:53), for example, in his discussion of Hausa in Ibadan, observes that intermarriage between Sabo men and Yoruba women could be highly subversive of Sabo ethnic exclusiveness, and so fatal to Hausa economic interests; he also shows how certain beliefs about the mystical dangers which can afflict the Hausa male who enters on such a mixed union serve to control the situation. Cohen here is hewing closely to his own line of analysis, but he is also following a respectable and fruitful anthropological tradition in focussing on marriage in its political aspects. Sabo, however, is a relatively small community with a high degree of internal organization and a coherent group ideology so that group pressures can be exerted against those who threaten to break the code, and are likely to be fairly effective. Elsewhere, however, the situation may well be different either in regard to ideology, to the degree of pressure that can be exerted, or both. On the Gazelle Peninsula, for example, the vast majority of Tolai marriages are intra-ethnic and, even though a good deal is heard nowadays about the freedom of individuals to choose their own partners, most unions continue to be parochial and consistent with established patterns of alliance (Epstein 1969:208-15). At the same time there is a small but growing number of Tolai who have found a spouse among other Papuan or New Guinean groups. At Matupit I encountered no antipathy to such marriages, [56] perhaps because in nearly all cases the alien partner settled on the island and was absorbed into the community, so that inter-marriage was not seen as posing any threat. On the Copperbelt the situation in regard to marriage has long been confused because of the difficulty in distinguishing between 'proper' and irregular marriages, because of the impermanent nature of many unions, whether 'proper' or otherwise, and the relative ease with which the parties moved from one kind of consortium to another (see Epstein 1953). While close kin are regarded as having formal status in the marriages of their wards, it is apparent that control of marriage on the Copperbelt is weak, and that choice of partner becomes much more a matter of individual preference. Nevertheless, it is interesting to note that choice operates within certain limits; a high proportion of marriages are still contracted within the ethnic group (see Mitchell 1957). A further point of interest to emerge from Mitchell's preliminary findings is that the pattern of in- and out-marriage varies considerably from one group to another. Clearly, as was suggested earlier, ethnicity on the Copperbelt may mean different things for different groups.

It should also be noted here that the child of an inter-ethnic Copperbelt union does not cease to have a 'tribal' identity. During my fieldwork I only encountered one man who, because of his very mixed descent, was genuinely unable to say to what tribe he belonged. Similarly, in America the case of the *mischling* indicates how there too it may be difficult to escape the net of ethnicity; as Glazer and Moynihan (1963:16) put it, neither Jews nor non-Jews will let them rest in ambiguity. Yet if escape is difficult, the opportunities that American society offers for social and spatial mobility ensure that escape does occur, and on a considerable scale. It is this possibility that underlines the concern among Jewish parents, amounting at times to a preoccupation, with the question of intermarriage. The point is documented in the Lakeville as well as other studies. Berman (1968:236), for example, poses the problem by citing the experience of a rabbi: 'What impels Jewish parents to oppose intermarriage?' the rabbi asks.

'They seldom enter a synagogue from one year to the next. They do not observe the dietary laws or any of the ritual of Jewish life. Their relationship to the Jewish community is only nominal ... Why do they get so disturbed about the possibility of their son or daughter marrying a non-Jew? They sit before me with tears in their eyes and literally cry out, "Rabbi, you've got to save my child."'

Berman himself offers an explanation for this kind of behaviour when in a later context (p. 309) he points out that what at first sight seems uncanny, unreasonable, and illiberal, becomes quite understandable when viewed as a by-product of that most familiar Jewish norm: group solidarity. In much the same way, discussing the attitude adopted towards intermarriage by leaders of Reform Judaism, who have shown themselves unable to accept the logic of their own integrationist ideology, Glazer (1972:55) explains the anomaly by what he calls a simple unreflecting attachment to the Jewish people, a subconscious insistence that the Jews be maintained as a people.

Such responses to the threat of intermarriage reveal from one point of view the affective power of ethnicity at its most naked. From another perspective, however, they also point to the no less powerful pull of other forces present in the environment, and to the problems of boundary maintenance in a society where relations between ethnic groups are not formally defined within the social structure. For the crisis in these cases arises precisely because the parents were unsuccessful in transmitting their own attachment to the group, expressed chiefly in affective terms, to their children. To say this is not of course to dispose of affect as an important component of ethnicity. It is merely to recognize that the force which attaches one to a particular group is not transmitted in the genes; it has to be created anew in each succeeding generation. What is at issue here, therefore, is the way in which the sense of ethnic identity is perpetuated.

Erikson (1968:41) has coined the term *pseudo-species* to express the way throughout human history groups of various kinds have emerged and bound their members in loyalty by developing, within a territorial framework, their own body of custom, mythology and rite, and history. Hence, where neighbouring ethnic groups have been in stable interaction through time, their cultural differences, however subtle these may appear to the outsider, serve in themselves as effective boundary-markers. In the situations with which I have been concerned here, however, the problem is very different, for all are characteristically marked by a high degree of cultural erosion and the disappearance of many expressions of distinctiveness. We touch here on what seems to me to be one of the most crucial issues in the discussion of ethnicity, but one which has been least studied and which is least understood. The problem strikes me as having two important aspects, and I shall seek to explore each of them further in the essays which follow. Here I confine myself to some preliminary remarks.

In approaching the first aspect — the categorical — it may be helpful to remind ourselves of the duality that attaches to ethnicity, that ethnic identity, as I have argued, is the product of the interplay of internal and external factors. Each situation in which we encounter ethnicity will vary therefore in accordance with the nature of the balance struck between these factors. I have tried to show how, using material from the Copperbelt and New Guinea, new ethnic categories come to be generated. But what also emerges from this material, which I will discuss again further in the next essay, is the way in which ethnicity quickly becomes intimately interwoven with questions of hierarchy, stratification, and the pursuit of political interests. In these circumstances the categories quickly become 'social facts' in the Durkheimian sense, increasingly taking on a life of their own, from which it may be extremely difficult for the individual to escape. Identity, I have suggested, always involves a measure of choice, but here it operates within severe constraints, though these may vary in their intensity as between different groups. In such contexts then the persistence of ethnicity owes more to the pressures from without; in so far as people interact and compete with one another in terms of ethnic categories the extent to which they adhere to customary beliefs and practices becomes irrelevant; one's response to those of another group is apt to be governed by negative sterotypes. Mobilization in defence of ethnic interests may not always lead to a process of 'retribalization' such as Cohen (1969) has described for the Hausa of Sabo. At the same time the fact that a set of 'external' categories is being constantly employed is likely to prompt a response from within, leading to a stress on, or attachment to, some forms of behaviour that will come to serve as symbols of exclusiveness; these in turn intensify and reinforce the sense of identity. So, among the Tolai, the outside observer is bound to be struck by the remarkable persistence of their shell-money in circumstances where the pressures working against it over many years might have led one to expect its disappearance long ago. Young people who are in full-time wage employment continue to make strenuous efforts to acquire *tambu* for bride-wealth payments or to observe the proper obsequies on the death of parents and other kin: without *tambu*, they say, as noted earlier, 'we would not be Tolai, we would be another people'. *Tambu* has thus come to serve as a primary symbol of Tolai identity; that in recent years it has also become for some the focus of a fierce ambivalence points no less clearly to the crisis of Tolai identity described already.[57] In the absence of a systematic investigation, the situation on the Copperbelt is less easy to describe; what does seem clear is that inner perceptions and responses differ as between one ethnic group and another, as well as within them, reflecting the nature of the total structure and the position of the different groups within it. The American scene differs from both of these in a number of important respects. In America too, of course, ethnicity is closely bound up with social stratification and differential access to resources, but even though the categories have an independent force of their own the social system does provide greater opportunities for individuals to discard their ethnic identity and merge themselves in the ranks of the dominant white middle class. In such circumstances, for certain categories at least, one's identity becomes much more a matter of personal choice, and the perpetuation of the ethnic identity must come to depend increasingly on the strength of inner resources, on the contribution from within.

The question what form this contribution can take leads me to the second aspect of the problem: the role of custom or symbol in the transmission of identity. It is true of course that practices discarded in one generation can be revived in the next, and in fact this occurs not infrequently. However, the point I have in mind is a rather different one. I have spoken from time to time of cultural erosion, and while the evidence for this process is abundantly clear, it also occurs to me that it may be important to distinguish between what I may term 'public' culture and 'intimate' culture. I have noted earlier that most of the studies of ethnicity in America with which I am familiar were conducted by way of interviewing a sample of respondents rather than by participant observation. In measuring the strength of ethnic attachment, therefore, researchers have tended to focus on the extent to which particular customs continue to be followed or not; such traits can be readily itemized and quantified. What such studies show frequently then is how many of the practices that were once acknowledged as important elements of the 'traditional' way of life of the group, its 'public' culture, have come to be abandoned in varying degree. Two interconnected points need to be noted here. First, there is the assumption that underlies these research procedures that the persistence of custom holds the key to the persistence of identity. Such a view stands in need of some qualification, for as Blau (1965:111) has observed of Jewish orthodoxy, 'a strict adherence to every detail of ritual and personal practice may be an expression of profound piety and of a keen spiritual sense of the sanctity of every experience of every day. It may equally well be the husk that remains when the kernel has rotted.' What would seem to be important in the transmission of identity is not practice in itself, but the meaning that attaches to it, and the way it is cathected. Such issues have rarely been the concern of sociological inquiry into ethnicity. This leads directly to the second point. For, following the same line of thought, one is led to suspect that many of the subtler expressions of ethnic behaviour that are revealed in the ongoing life of the home, in the company of friends, or at ethnic gatherings, expressions of what I have called the 'intimate' culture, similarly escape the sociologist's net. One's suspicion that this is so is heightened by the fact, for example, that American Jews have consistently displayed certain social characteristics that have distinguished them from other ethnic groups within the population: the importance attached to schooling and higher education, the low incidence of alcoholism or delinquency, or the stability of family life, and so on (see, e.g. Glazer 1965). However such facts are to be explained, what they reveal is that American Jews continue to display in their behaviour certain values and attitudes despite their abandonment of much of their 'public' culture. They suggest too that such values are cultivated and transmitted as part of the 'intimate' culture. Rather than focussing on custom as such we are thus prompted to search for these values and attitudes as they are manifested in 'intimate' situations. In studying how they are transmitted to and experienced by the young we may hope to discover how the cognitive aspects of identity are buttressed by unconscious associations and identifications, and so come to a deeper understanding of the affective component of ethnic identity.

In drawing attention to the importance of childhood experience in ethnic identity-formation I am not arguing for a simple psychological model to explain ethnicity, as I hope my earlier reference to the mother-child bond makes clear. In a paper entitled 'Why Ethnicity?' Glazer and Moynihan (1974) note two poles of analysis in recent approaches to the problem: the 'primordialist' and the 'circumstantialist'. The first stresses the affective components in identity-formation, the second adopts a sociological stance and concentrates on the way social circumstances influence degrees of ethnic attachment, mobilization, and conflict. Between these poles, they observe, explanations for the persistence or revival or creation of ethnic identities tend to waver — their own included. In this essay I hope to have avoided this dilemma by regarding 'affect' and 'circumstance' not as variables to be handled separately, but to be treated in their complex interaction. For certain purposes it may be valid, and even useful, to stress one aspect at the expense of the other. But if we are to achieve a deeper understanding of many of the problems that ethnicity poses, we shall need to develop methods and approaches more fine-grained than those adopted hitherto which takes full account of the interplay of the external and the internal, the objective and the subjective, and the sociological and psychological elements which are always present in the formation of ethnic identity.

## 2. MILITARY ETHOS AND ETHNIC RANKING ON THE COPPERBELT

In my previous essay I took the view that the perception of the self, and the ways in which that perception is made manifest in behaviour, are always in some measure an expression of one's relations with others. I also noted that since as members of society we are involved with no one single category of significant others, but with a number of such categories, each of us holds simultaneously a number of identities. This can be a source of conflict, but often this is so successfully contained that the individual may go through much of his life without being made consciously aware of it. The identifications one makes, for example, with the village or town in which one lives, with the country, province, or region within which it is set, and with the wider nation may at times involve a clash of loyalties, but for the most part they form a series in which the different identities 'nest' within a hierarchy, and mutually reinforce one another, the social context determining which identity shall be stressed. On the other hand, it is also plain that the more varied the bases of social grouping, the greater the potential for identity-conflict and the more difficult its containment. Accordingly it is always important in discussions of ethnicity to see ethnic identity as one among a number of alternative and possibly competing, identities; it has to be understood, that is to say, in the context of relations between ethnic and other categories within a particular social environment. One of the reasons that ethnicity has acquired its contemporary salience in modern and modernizing states is that so often it has become intimately interwoven with issues of dominance, hierarchy, and stratification. By way of leading into a discussion of such questions as they have arisen on the Copperbelt of Zambia, I have chosen to focus on a problem which, so far as my knowledge goes, has received little or no treatment in the general literature. I refer here to the way in which a tradition of a military past, brought into being under particular historical circumstances, has persisted into the very changed conditions of today. In particular, I am concerned with the way the tradition, and the values associated with it, enter into the definition of relations between different ethnic groups.

Let me begin by trying to define the problem a little more precisely. In my earlier study of Luanshya (Epstein 1958:6) I quoted at one point the remarks once made to Audrey Richards by some African women when she was visiting Broken Hill (now Kabwe). The Bemba and the Ngoni, these women declared, were the only tribes whose women still desired to have many children and to build up families. It was because of their aristocracy, the women explained. What Richards's informants clearly intended to imply was that the two groups still maintained a sense of pride from the past; they continued to display their feelings of superiority over the groups by their refusal to deny traditional values and to succumb to the corrupting influences of the towns. These views in turn harked back to the status of Bemba and Ngoni as ruling groups, groups which in the pre-colonial era had established their dominance and suzerainty over other tribes of the region by military conquest. I followed this quotation from Richards with a footnote reference to the verse of a song that was chanted by Bemba when they performed their *mbeni* dance. Translated from Bemba the verse runs:

The Compound Manager asks: show me the tribe here in Luanshya
In Luanshya show me the tribe.
Number One — Bemba!
Number Two — Ngoni!
These people are 'saini ofu'.

'Saini ofu' is one of those typical expressions of the modern argot that has developed on the Copperbelt (see Epstein 1959). I did not discover its precise etymology, though it clearly derives from English. My suspicion is that it refers to a man who is prepared to lose his job, i.e., sign off, rather than accept meekly some indignity at the hands of a European in a position of authority. That at any rate would be consistent with the meaning of the expression given to me by Africans: to be utterly without fear. And here again the reference to the military values of the past, and the way they enter into contemporary behaviour, is quite plain.

Among some mining officials on the Copperbelt Bemba had a reputation for truculence, and were said to be less amenable to discipline than other sections of the African labour force. But such judgments can hardly be taken at face value. Those Bemba with whom I discussed the matter would deny the charge vigorously and claim in turn that mine officials tended to describe any African worker who was troublesome as a Bemba because such a high proportion of the work force came from the Northern Province, and the officials were too idle or too ignorant to distinguish between one group and another. Statements of these kinds which might have a bearing on the possible relationship between contemporary behaviour and a former martial tradition can neither be unequivocally refuted or confirmed because it is not possible to produce rates showing the incidence of truculence or similar behaviour traits for the different ethnic groups represented in the Copperbelt African population. Similarly, a relationship of the kind asserted by the women with whom Richards talked in Broken Hill is not easily susceptible of proof; there is in fact no evidence that fertility rates among Bemba and Ngoni differ significantly from those of other groups,[1] but even if they did it might prove difficult to identify the causal factor(s). In these instances then we are not dealing with objective group characteristics; such statements are of interest rather for what they tell us of people's perceptions of their new environment, how they come to structure it, and to interpret their various experiences and observations within it. However, there is an area of social life where one can readily detect that a tradition embodying a complex of values centring around former military prowess does continue to exist in meaningful ways. This relates to the ways in which particular groups define themselves. Any act of self-definition projects an image of the (group) self, but, as I have previously argued, just as any image of the self refracts some aspects of one's relations with others, so here, for example, Bemba views of themselves are also an expression of their relations with other groups.

The problem which I began by raising thus has two aspects. At first glance it would seem that a tradition of former military glory can have little relevance in the setting of a modern industrial habitat. The Bemba or Ngoni who are to be found among the work force of a coppermine are not there as warriors, nor even as the grandsons of warriors, but as urban workers; we would not ordinarily expect that a man would be placed in a position of authority or given a higher-status job simply because he belongs to a once-conquering tribe. On the contrary, the African on the Copperbelt quickly discovers that he has to work together with, and in some cases to accept orders from, individuals of tribes which his own group had once defeated in battle. In many other cases he is in close contact with persons belonging to groups with which his own had simply had no social relationship in the past. In such circumstances we are led to ask first why a people like the Bemba should continue, while in town, to emphasize their military past in defining themselves *vis-à-vis* other groups. The second, and in a way more interesting, question is why other groups, lacking this tradition of military success, perhaps even the victims of aggression in the past, should operate with the same sets of evaluations so that, as I shall discuss presently, reputation in warfare has come to provide an important criterion in the development of a system of ethnic ranking on the Copperbelt.

But before turning to this matter, in order to dispel any impression that I am talking here of ethnic identity in purely psychological and ahistorical terms (see Magubane 1969), let me focus briefly on the Bemba to see how their military record contributed to their sense of tribal identity in the past. Audrey Richards and all the other ethnographers of the Bemba have regularly and consistently referred to the emphasis on military values in Bemba culture. When earlier observers, entering the country in the 1890s, noted a lesser concern with agriculture among the Bemba than was the case with some of their neighbours, and taxed them on the matter, they received the reply: 'Our gardens are over there.' The informants were pointing in the direction of Mambwe country. From such accounts it might appear that raiding and warfare had been a defining characteristic of Bemba life from the very beginning. However, the recent work of historians, such as

Roberts (1974), makes it clear that any judgment about the nature of Bemba culture that is rooted in the assumption of a relatively static society must be open to serious question. Thus it is now plain that the Bemba polity that Richards first began to describe in the 1930s only came into being in the fifty years or so prior to the British entry into the region and the establishment there of the *pax britannica*. Around the turn of the nineteenth century the Bemba were a rather small group inhabiting the areas of a few chiefdoms in what are now the Kasama and Chinsali Districts, areas which even today are still thought of as the true heart of Bemba country and whose people are spoken of as the only 'true Bemba' (*BaBemba nkonko*). Then, somewhere around 1830, in the reign of Chitimukulu Chileshye (?1827-1860), there began a remarkable transformation. By the time the British arrived in the 1890s the Bemba held sway over almost the entire Great Plateau, and Bemba chiefs and headmen were now installed as rulers over vast tracts of country which only a little earlier had acknowledged their own traditional leaders.

I have recently examined this development in some detail elsewhere (Epstein 1975) and, in seeking to account for it, drew particular attention to the importance of the changing character of Bemba military organization. The point that is of immediate interest for present purposes is that while it is possible, even likely, that in the remoter past Bemba had raided and fought with their neighbours, during the reign of Chileshye warfare began to take on quite a different complexion. One aspect of the new situation that merits special comment here was the mounting ferocity, reaching its peak in the reign of Chitimukulu Chitapankwa (c.1860-1883), with which the Bemba waged war. Sheane (1911:23), for example, reports an episode from the wars against the Bisa when the Bemba 'wreaked their vengeance upon Matipa and his people until they were tired of slaughter, and long after the Bisa had acknowledged themselves the slaves of Mwamba'. Nor was this an isolated incident, for engagements with other groups also finished up with systematic slaughter despite the fact that the enemy had surrendered. Plainly, warfare conducted in this fashion was no longer a matter of petty raiding, to pillage or to take booty in the form of cattle; it was now tied to more clearly political aims — the conquest, control, and settlement of new areas.

The incursion into the region of the Ngoni, an offshoot of the martial Zulu, also occurred during Chileshye's reign, and Chileshye had the greatest difficulty in containing them. These difficulties may help to account for the fact that the Bemba were not able to maintain effective control of Bisa country which the Portuguese explorer Gamitto, who reached the Court of Mwata Kazembe of the Lunda in 1831, reported they had earlier conquered. In fact it was only in the reign of Chitapankwa that the Ngoni were finally expelled from Bemba country. Thereafter there was no effective opposition from other groups and the Bemba were able to embark on a series of wars of expansion with the results already noted.

Martial values were certainly a part of Bemba culture before Chitapankwa, but the available evidence also suggests very strongly that it was Chitapankwa who really developed the warlike character of the Bemba and brought these values to their full flowering. Under Chitapankwa bravery became a prime social virtue. From boyhood Bemba lads were trained to the sight of blood by calling them out to greet the warriors returning from battle. They were required to relieve the soldiers of the severed heads of the enemy they had slain and to carry them into the village. Those who performed the task without blenching were rewarded with privileges normally reserved only for their seniors. Acts of valour in war were rewarded with gifts from the King and respect among the people. The man who returned from an engagement with wounds in his chest was acclaimed; the man who was wounded in the back was punished. Cowardice was not tolerated.

There is another aspect of Bemba military policy which has a direct bearing on my present theme. Warfare, I have said, was now being waged with great ferocity, a development that is at once reminiscent of the Zulu under Chaka. Like the Zulu, the Bemba too spared none. After the taking of a village, the male captives were either sold into slavery or were simply butchered. Women too were also sold as slaves, but many were given instead as wives to Bemba soldiers who settled in the newly acquired areas. Since most of the peoples whom the Bemba fought and defeated followed the rule of matrilineal descent, it might be expected that the offspring of these unions would retain the tribal identity and allegiance of their mothers. What happened in fact was that they tended to identify rather with their more prestigious and conquering fathers. I suspect that this process of identification was also encouraged by another feature of the changing Bemba political and social system.

As elsewhere, conquest had important implications for the system of social stratification. Military values provided the basis for a system of ranking, a framework within which all sections of the population could measure their relative social position. At the top of course was the King, the epitome of those values and the lynch-pin of the whole system, followed by the hereditary councillors or *bakabilo* and military officers (*bamushika*) who acted as his confidantes and advisers. The position of the Bemba commoners was itself elevated by the presence of the newly subject peoples and slaves. What needs to be stressed here however, is that, unlike the situation that developed in some other parts of Africa, Bemba conquest did not give rise to a system of castes based on the dichotomy of victors and vanquished. On the contrary, Bemba society was in certain respects a remarkably open one in which military prowess and distinction could open up the path to social advancement. Even a slave, it was said, could rise to be a *mushika*, a senior officer in the army. In these ways, then, very large areas of the countryside were very rapidly and effectively Bembaized; the conquered were successfully merged in a common Bemba identity.

This is not the occasion for a discussion of the nature of pre-colonial polity of the Bemba. There are a few points, however, relevant to my present concerns, that should be noted. First, it is important to stress than when full allowance has been made for the considerable achievements of Chitapankwa in binding so many groups into some semblance of cohesion, the simple fact remains that he did not succeed in creating the machinery of a unitary state that he could bequeath to his successors. Indeed, within a short time of his death the fabric of the kingdom was being rent by serious internal divisions. When, not very long afterwards, the Europeans began to appear on the scene, although the Bemba were still engaged in waging war on their neighbours, the signs of internal cleavage were all too evident. Unlike the Ngoni, whom they had earlier repulsed, the Bemba, for so many years the scourge of the Great Plateau, yielded to the British almost without a struggle. One can only speculate what might have happened had the British not intervened at this point. One possibility is that the precarious unity achieved under Chitapankwa might have been completely sundered, and the group as a whole splintered along its various lines of cleavage. But such speculation in this instance is idle and unfruitful, for what happened in fact was that with the imposition of the *pax britannica* the system of group relations that had been in the process of development on the Great Plateau, and was still in a state of considerable flux, was suddenly frozen. Although formal recognition of indigenous institutions in line with the policy of indirect rule still lay in the far-off future, and although there were numerous features of the Bemba system of which the new colonial authorities disapproved and sought to remove or change, the Administration had perforce to make use of what was to hand. To this extent the Bemba quickly became a 'tribe' within a wider political and administrative system. In a sense the colonial regime had brought a new group into being and through the very workings of the system helped to perpetuate it. At the same time recognition of this fact should not blind us to the importance of noting how the new situation presented itself to the people themselves. And what is crucial here, I believe, is that the new identity that the Bemba had been developing had been forged in the fires of war. For certain segments of the population, the Chitimukulu himself, the members of the Crocodile clan, and the hereditary *bakabilo*, the continuity of the group might be expressed in the myths of origin which told of the departure of the first Chiti and his followers from distant Kola, and which provided a charter for their traditionally prescribed roles as well as for many of their ritual activities. But for the vast majority of the population in the heyday of Bemba expansion to be a Bemba was to be associated with a powerful and prestigious group whose success was built up around an efficient military organization, which had in turn contributed to the development of a sharply emphasized military ethos. It is with the persistence of this kind of identity, and the values associated with it, in the towns of the Copperbelt that we are presently concerned.

I have just mentioned how myths, and the various rituals and other activities which translate myth into social reality, contribute to the group's sense of its own continuity. But what are we to understand by continuity? Though the term is frequently invoked, it has not, so far as I am aware, received a great deal of critical attention in the anthropological literature. However, one attempt to define the notion, and to apply it consistently, that of the Wilsons (1954), is of particular interest here because their analysis relied upon observations and a long experience both in the rural and urban areas of Central Africa. As the Wilsons formulate it, continuity lies in the volume of material co-operation and communication with the past, and the non-material unity that exists when people act, speak, and feel as if it were a reality. This non-material reality, they then proceed to argue, is differently defined in different types of society. Thus tribal peoples are said to define it as cultural similarity, stressing observance of the same customs as were practised by their forefathers. In modern societies, by contrast, it is development that is stressed — there is held to be a certain continuity between, say, feudalism and later constitutional government, not because such regimes are alike, but because one grew out of the other. On either of these criteria it is evident that contemporary African life on the Copperbelt is marked by a high degree of discontinuity. Thus if we focus on such major domains of social life as economics, politics, or religion the overriding impression is one of sharp contrasts rather than of 'cultural similarity'; it is less so in the realm of kinship, though this should not be allowed to conceal the fact that kinship too operates in the towns in ways significantly at variance with the way it did in traditional rural society. Where military organization is concerned the matter is perhaps the most clear-cut of all, for the contemporary urban milieu offers little scope for the formal expression of this particular aspect of pre-colonial tribal life. Viewing continuity as a process of development yields a similar result, for it is difficult to see how one can adequately describe those institutions and other social arrangements characteristic of African life on the Copperbelt as having developed out of tribal ones.[2] Analytically, the Wilsons' distinction seems unhelpful and indeed misleading because, following the method of polar contrast which they appear to have taken over from Durkheim, their formulation of the concept of continuity ignores the fact that there is an element in the situation common to all types of society be they rural or urban, 'primitive' or modern. The Wilsons miss this point because they have lumped together, and so confused, the perspectives of the actor and the outside observer.

In pursuing this point it may be helpful to resort to an analogy. From the various orifices with which our bodies are provided it is evident that matter continually enters and leaves the human frame, and we now recognize that change is going on all the time. The whole cellular structure is being broken down and replaced as it matures so that, as Campbell (1967:17) put it, the same body in infancy and old age has little in common beyond its genotype and a dynamic system of a particular kind. Campbell adds that human personality, the continuing identifiable nature of an individual, is one aspect of this system; another, which he does not discuss, is the individual's perception of himself as essentially the same person in spite of all the changes he has experienced, his ego-identity. So, too, if we consider the individual in his social aspect, as a member of society, we observe again a continuous process of change as he moves from one status to another, and yet withal remaining identifiable as the same person. Similar processes are at work in human groups. I refer to the identifiable thread of continuity of a group as its ethos, the structure of assumptions, values, and meanings which underlie particular and varying expressions of cultural behaviour; and just as in the case of the individual the notion of personality is accompanied at the level of self-perception by the sense of ego-identity, so ethos has as its counterpart the sense of collective identity, the consciousness of belonging to a group that exists in time.

Many factors contribute to fostering such a sense of collective identity. Continuing attachment to land provides one of the most obvious examples, and where ethnic groups are concerned territory nearly always, perhaps even universally, turns out to have great significance, positive or negative, for identity formation. Or it may be the sharing of a language or literary heritage, a religion, a common historical fate, or some combination of these. Such factors merge with, and serve to feed, the sense of history, that thread which links a people or a group to its past and holds its promise for the future. In speaking of history I should perhaps hasten to add that I do not use the term here in the sense employed by a professional historian who is concerned to study the detailed interrelationships of events within some temporal framework. For many Englishmen, the story, for example, of Joan of Arc is one they will have heard at school, and few will be familiar with its details and complexities. They would probably also be surprised to discover that the story is presented quite differently in French school textbooks. History from this point of view embraces a scheme of values seen from the perspective of a particular group at a given moment of time. History, moreover, is selective; the richer the historical fabric the greater the potential for selection and reinterpretation, while yet maintaining the sense of continuity. As values or social situations change, so history too changes. Hence, while one can agree with the Wilsons that history is of major importance in defining and helping to perpetuate a sense of group continuity, it must be stressed that it is not simply by providing a record of change and development that it achieves this. If, for example, Englishmen feel some sense of unity with their Tudor or Elizabethan ancestors it is not simply because their present society is seen to have grown out of feudalism through a complex historical process, but rather because they are able to identify with their forebears as being in some respects the same people, in spite of the great structural changes that have overtaken English society in recent centuries. It is in this regard, in presenting a sense of familiarity in what would otherwise appear remote, that continuity provides the basis for a national or ethnic identity, a perception of the group self which has been fostered by history, the values it enshrines and the symbols through which it has been transmitted. In these same elements we find some of the sources of that powerful affect that so often mark the expression of group identity, its capacity to elicit deep feelings of attachment and loyalty. Nor should one overlook in this context how, as I have discussed earlier, both at the individual and group levels, identity is intimately connected with notions of worthiness, pride, dignity, and manhood.

Against the background of this discussion let me now return to the Copperbelt. As I have mentioned, the urban industrial environment offers little scope for the expression of ethnic chauvinism, particularly a brand that is based on former martial glories; such matters can have little relevance within the framework of a system that stresses differentiation in terms of productive roles. On the other hand, represented within the Copperbelt population there are a number of groups, such as Bemba and Ngoni, whose sense of ethnic identity is closely linked to their military record in pre-colonial days. In so far then as ethnic identity is bound up with a sense of continuity with the past, the first question that arises is to what extent, and in what contexts, that sense of continuity finds an outlet in the urban milieu. Unfortunately, as so often throughout these essays, I only became alive to the problem long after I had completed my fieldwork, and my data are as far from systematic as I could wish. Even so, I think I can point to a number of situations, both at the personal and group levels, where the fact that one belongs to a group with a martial tradition continues to be meaningful.

I take first an example where such attitudes are reflected in the behaviour of an individual. Early in my fieldwork at Luanshya, at a gathering of Africans at the home of the District Commissioner, I was introduced to a man whom I shall call John Mutale. Mutale was one of the most prominent Africans in the town, indeed on the Copperbelt as a whole; apart from serving on many local bodies he was a member of the African Representative Council and was considered by many as a serious candidate for the Legislative Council which had at that time four African members. He was a man of great personal charm and integrity and spoke impeccable English in spite of the limitations of his formal education; on completing standard six at primary school he had taken a teacher's training course before joining the mine as a clerk and interpreter. In short, he was an outstanding representative of that new class of Africans of his day, seemingly a complete product of the society that had grown up around the mine townships. Mutale had already been told of my earlier stay in Bemba country and of my familiarity, undoubtedly exaggerated in the telling, with Bemba language and culture, and within a short time of our introduction he volunteered this remark: 'You will of course understand what I am about to tell you. I am a grandson of Mubanga Chipoya.' This was a reference to the Bemba chief Mwamba III, sometimes known as Mwamba the Great, whose reputation as a warrior was second only to that of Chitimukulu Chitapankwa, who was his mother's brother. Such an item of information would have meant little to the District Commissioner, who had never served in Bemba country, and even less to other Europeans with whom Mutale was in contact. He mentioned it to me because he assumed that I would appreciate what lay behind it, and because presumably he hoped that I would be impressed. He would hardly have done so, however, if he himself had not attached importance to the fact. He was expressing in this way pride in his lineage and tradition, so that for Mutale being Bemba was clearly an important part of his personal identity, a fact that was not ordinarily apparent in one's observations of much of his public behaviour.

There are other contexts of a formal kind where Bemba publicly assert their ethnic pride. I have referred earlier to the *mbeni* dance. In its basic characteristics *mbeni* has much in common with the *Kalela* dance so well described by Mitchell, and both indeed seem to derive from a common source (Mitchell 1956:9). But there are also some interesting points of difference. Mitchell described *Kalela* as a 'tribal' dance because it emphasized the unity of Bisa against all other tribes on the Copperbelt, but he was also at pains to point out that it did so by stressing familiar urban themes and situations, and not by reference back to a Bisa past. *Mbeni* too makes use of contemporary themes, but it is the explicit emphasis on a military past which is immediately striking. Thus in the middle of the dance-yard there is a tall flag-pole on which a 'flag', referred to as *ilamfya*, is hung. The 'flag' is a piece of cloth moulded to the shape of *ilamfya*, the war-horn always carried in the van when the Bemba marched into battle (see Epstein 1975). The martial theme is also evident in a verse chanted by the dancers which I quoted at the outset. Here are a few others in similar vein:

> What are you gazing at?
> Child, that thing swinging there
> Is the *ilamfya* horn,
> The hawk which tears with its beak,
> That plucks out the eyes.

> The country they gave Chitapankwa has grown very large indeed,
> Very large indeed
> Even Lamba country itself
> And even the Kaonde, the Swaka, and Kalwena are Bemba.

> For this thing you have done,
> Father John, be careful of them.
> You have cut down the swinging 'flag'.
> Do you not know these Bemba pluck out the eyes?[3]

One would expect to find the attitudes reflected in these verses given behavioural expression in contexts other than the dance arena, and the fact that Bemba are commonly regarded as arrogant and boastful suggests that this may be so. Since these attitudes are presumably inculcated, or at least acquired, in the course of one's early upbringing, study of their expression in the behaviour of the young might be particularly profitable. I do not know at what age a child becomes aware of himself as a member of a particular tribe, but I was often struck by the fact that the veriest tot would have no difficulty in identifying himself when I would ask playfully *uli mutundu nshi?* (What tribe are you?) It would also be of considerable interest to know what ethnic identity is assumed by the offspring of inter-ethnic unions. In dealing with disputes arising out of such unions, particularly where the question of custody of the children was concerned, the African Urban Courts tended to adopt the position that 'a man enters the customs of the woman', so that in this predominantly matrilineal country children take on the ethnic identity of their mothers. It appears, however, that outside the purview of the courts this principle is not always followed in practice. I have mentioned earlier how in the heyday of Bemba expansion children would identify with their conquering and more prestigious fathers, and I have sometimes chanced upon a similar kind of phenomenon on the Copperbelt. There was, for example, a Bemba man who had married a Tumbuka woman from Malawi. Once, meeting a kinswoman of his wife, the Bemba introduced his young son to her saying 'this is your mother'. The child immediately protested: 'No, no that woman is speaking ChiNgoni. I am a Bemba.' What is especially interesting about this case is that the father, who had been brought up from early boyhood on the Copperbelt, and was now a leading official of the African National Congress, was normally quick to condemn any manifestation of what he saw as 'tribalism' and he claimed to attach little importance to the fact that he himself was Bemba.

The child in this instance was of pre-school age. By the time children on the Copperbelt are ready to go to school it seems that the sense of ethnic identity is already firmly established, and influences their behaviour there. Although J did not carry out systematic observations in the schools I did visit them from time to time, had discussions with many teachers, and sometimes had the students write essays for me as part of their regular work on different topics in which I was interested. From this information it appeared that friendship sets among schoolchildren were formed on a variety of bases: neighbourhood, the common class background of the parents, or the sharing of 'gang' interests as in gambling or the smoking of dagga. Tribal ties were another important factor in social interaction, and some groups were said to be more 'cliquey' than others. On occasion ethnic attitudes were even carried into the classroom, and I was told by one headmaster how sometimes a boy summoned to the front of the class would be hooted with stereotyped taunts relating to his tribe. Two contrasting sets of attitudes are reflected in the following extracts from essays on the theme 'what my tribe means to me'. The first is by a Bemba, and reads:

'My tribe to me means it is unlimited wealth given by God. Secondly, it means that I must know to where I belong. There are many people who think that their tribe means nothing to them. When they hear people laughing at their tribe they get ashamed, they think that their tribe is not important, and gradually they stop speaking of their tribe and begin to speak of another which they think is an important one. Such people are foolish because they don't think that their tribe is a great gift from God.'

The second comes from an essay written by a Lamba student:

'I have found no reason why some people say that tribe is something of great importance in the world. Myself, I am greatly opposed to this because I have seen nothing of what they have done to their tribes. I remember one of my classmates in standard 4. He was a very handsome boy, a MuBemba from Chinsali. But he used to laugh at my tribe and I asked him why he was fond of laughing, and he did not hide the truth. He said because your tribe is too low compared to his. Then I told him that we must fight now with our brains and see who will be successful in the government examinations. When we did our examinations, we assembled in the hall, and I saw that my friend had failed. Then I asked him that you are still proud of your tribe. He said no, because he knew that he has disgraced his tribe for he has not passed.'

What emerges from all this is not simply that some individuals take pride in their ethnic background, or even seek to impress their superiority over others, but that there is also a general recognition, however much it may be resented in some cases, that some tribes are more 'important' than others. Formulating it in rather different terms, we may say that the notion of 'importance' has assumed something of the character of a 'social fact' in the Durkheimian sense in that individuals, whatever their personal views in the matter, are forced to take cognizance of it. I have mentioned the case of Mutale, a leading personality in Luanshya, who carried his Bemba identity with quiet pride. Consider now the rather different case of another man whom I shall call Mulenda. Mulenda was younger than Mutale, but in terms of his education, the style of life to which he aspired, and his general outlook, he too was similarly very much a product of the new urban society of the Copperbelt. But whereas Mutale always gave the appearance of being self-assured and at ease with himself and others, Mulenda was conspicuously lacking in these qualities. Although he enjoyed a certain status as the Secretary of one of the African trade unions based in the municipal location, Mulenda clearly felt that he did not receive the social recognition to which he considered he was properly entitled, and he frequently spoke to me of the obstacles to advancement that he encountered. He attributed these difficulties to the fact that he was a Lamba, a tribe, he observed, that was generally regarded on the Copperbelt as being without consequence. One might want to interpret such statements in terms of individual psychology, seeing Mulenda as a man unable to confront his own inadequacy and seeking its roots in sources outside himself. But that would hardly do justice to the facts, for if Mulenda was speaking out of self-pity he was also accurately reporting a certain facet of the Copperbelt social system. Once, for example, in conversation with an African Health Inspector I happened to ask the meaning of a Lamba word I had recently recorded in my notes. The man, a Bemba, said he did not know and added immediately that, anyway, it didn't matter because Lamba was not a language *lwa chiheavy*, a language that carried prestige. It becomes apparent that we are in the presence of a system of ethnic ranking where different groups are seen as being ordered in relation to one another in terms of some criterion of prestige.

What is this criterion, and what is it that makes one tribe more 'important' or 'heavy' than another? As I shall discuss shortly, more than one set of factors enters into the assessment. Let me focus first on the question of military tradition. It will be recalled that Mitchell's analysis of the *Kalela* dance included a discussion of the perception of social distance among different ethnic groups on the Copperbelt. The pattern that emerged from his data was broadly consistent with what one might have expected on the hypothesis that geographical propinquity and cultural similarity were the relevant considerations in the definition of ethnic categories. Yet there were a number of interesting anomalies that were not accounted for on these criteria. Mitchell (1956:27), therefore, felt obliged to introduce a third factor: some groups, he noted, had widely established reputations, some favourable, some unfavourable, which affected their position in the social distance scale. Some of these reputations, he added, were easy to explain, commenting that 'the military prowess of the Ngoni, Ndebele and Bemba has no doubt contributed to the general high ranking of these people throughout all scales'. Mitchell, in other words, assumes a tradition of former military glory as a source of rank, and appears to think that the matter calls for no further explanation beyond the fact that the most prestigious ethnic groups that have now emerged on the Copperbelt tend to coincide with what were the most powerful and dominant groups in pre-colonial days. But is the matter so unproblematic? We have seen how, for example, in the case of the Bemba, their sense of tribal identity is bound up in their former military record, and we have also seen how the perpetuation of that tradition in an urban milieu affords some individuals at the very least certain psychic gratifications — a feeling of superiority over others. But why should other groups, whom one supposes might be happy to see an end to such arrogance and presumptuousness, also employ on occasion the same kind of evaluation? Today, groups like the Bemba, the Ngoni, and the Lozi provide points of reference in the perception of ethnic ranking, and although these perceptions vary according to the particular perspective adopted, there is a good deal of overlap, suggesting widespread recognition of a fairly clear-cut ranking system. Why are the other groups prepared to accept the premises on which the system rests, and indeed make use themselves of those very same premises? In seeking answers to these questions, I want to suggest that two interrelated factors are operative. The first relates to the way in which the values associated with former dominance have been transposed to the urban context. The second relates to a point I have frequently emphasized: that in seeking to understand relations between ethnic groups we need to set them within the relevant total social environment, in this instance the framework provided by the colonial situation.

Many variables can influence the ethnic composition of urban populations and the position that different ethnic groups come to assume within the urban system. Distance and transportation are often of importance, and Mitchell (1973) has been able to show for the Copperbelt, for example, how they bear not only on the distribution of ethnic categories there, but also on the kind and degree of urban involvement of different groups. Looked at from this point of view, we are not surprised to discover that the towns of the Copperbelt quickly became attractive to the Bemba and their Bemba-speaking neighbours in the Northern Province, who were soon numerically preponderant there, that the capital, Lusaka, became a magnet for migrant workers from the Eastern Province, and that the nucleus of Livingstone's African population should be drawn from among the Lozi and other groups in the Southern Province (see McCulloch 1956). Strength of numbers readily converts into other expressions of dominance. Thus one of the clearest expressions of Bemba pre-eminence on the Copperbelt is the way the Bemba language established itself there, so that it has become almost a *lingua franca.* [4] Together with English, Bemba was the medium of instruction in the schools, a fact which could be a source of disadvantage for those who had to learn it as a second, or indeed third, language.[5] Bemba too was usually the vernacular used in the church services of African congregations, a fact which has at least on one occasion precipitated a split in the congregation along ethno-linguistic lines.

There are yet other contexts where numbers serve to define the 'importance' of a tribe. There were, for example, African Urban Courts in all the main towns. The Court in each case was composed of four or at most five court members, all appointed for their assumed expertise in African customary law. Clearly not all the tribes present in the population of a given town could be represented on the bench, and the Administration followed the practice of inviting certain Native Authorities in the rural areas whose members were thought to be most numerous in a town to send a nominee to become a court member there. For many years there was indeed fierce competition and much clamour among the different groups for representation on the Urban Courts (see Epstein 1953). Much of this agitation was unavailing, and merely highlighted the fact that some tribes were more regularly represented in the different Courts than others. Here then was yet another arena where certain groups, dominant in the past, could point to their continuing pre-eminence in the modern urban world, and others were compelled, however grudgingly, to recognize it.

However, as I noted earlier, past dominance was only one criterion by which Africans assessed the 'importance' of different ethnic groups. A second criterion of prestige, both at the individual and the group levels, related to success measured in terms of contemporary urban and industrial values. Mitchell and I (1959) have shown that Africans on the Copperbelt had developed a fairly clear-cut perception of the ranking of occupations. This ranking, we suggested, related to the degree to which the occupation called for the qualifications which would enable those in it to follow what' they considered to be a 'civilized' way of life. The social grading of occupations, that is to say, reflected the more generalized prestige system which manifested itself as the emulation of the way of life of the socially dominant Europeans. From this point of view it would be extremely interesting to discover whether there is any regularity in the way in which ethnic groups are distributed among the various occupations, and to see to what extent the prestige enjoyed by a group on one criterion is maintained when quite a different criterion is adopted. To this end I have set out in the following table some data from Clyde Mitchell's social survey of the Copperbelt which he has not yet published and which he has kindly put at my disposal.

In the kind of colonial economy that obtained in Northern Rhodesia, where the country's wealth was built up essentially around the mining of copper, the social stratification of the population as a whole is immediately marked by the strong coincidence of race, occupational skills, and economic rewards. At the time of my own fieldwork Africans as a whole occupied a clearly subordinate position within the occupational structure. In the mass they provided an essentially unskilled labour force, the vast majority being employed on the mines or in the townships in a range of jobs for which little or no formal education was required, and where such training as was needed was given or acquired on the spot. Because, moreover, Northern Rhodesia was a country of White settlement where few European households were without their servants a very high proportion of Africans were in domestic service — the third largest 'industry' in the country at the time — as cooks, 'house-boys' or 'garden-boys'. Among their fellow Africans domestics were regarded as a distinctive category with their own behavioural characteristics, sometimes referred to as *fya bukaboi*, the 'boy' way of life, and they served an interesting function as cultural mediators between Black and White. Nevertheless, this should not be allowed to hide the fact that they too belonged to the mass of the unskilled. All groups, therefore, show a substantial proportion of their members among the ranks of the unskilled and the lowest paid. However, the labour force also included a number in more skilled or semi-skilled jobs as well as a small category of white-collar workers. Although there had not yet developed an African bourgeoisie such as Kuper (1965) has described for South Africa made up of those trained in the professions of medicine, law, journalism, and the like, the white-collar workers represented the nucleus of an emerging middle class. There was then increasing occupational differentiation among Africans, but the differences among them were minor compared to the vast gulf which separated them in wealth and status from the Europeans. On the other hand, precisely because they occupied a common position at the lowest level of the social structure, Africans found it important to emphasize their internal distinctions. They did so in terms of the principle of 'identification with the aggressor', that is, they adopted the values of the dominant Europeans in assessing the prestige that attached to particular occupations. White-collar jobs ranked highest: they called for a degree of education, including the ability to speak English with some proficiency, they carried higher wages and so opened up the path to a 'civilized' way of life (cf. Mitchell 1960). Although the data presented in *Table 2* throw up many

Diagram 1    *Distribution of the Copperbelt African labour force in unskilled and white-collar occupations by ethnic group*

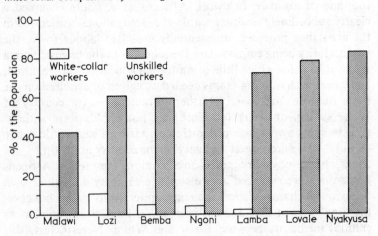

(*Source: Clyde Mitchell: Copperbelt Social Survey 1950-3*)

Table 2   Occupational Distribution of the Copperbelt African Labour Forms in Selected Ethnic Groups

| area of origin | ethnic group | occupations | | | | | | |
|---|---|---|---|---|---|---|---|---|
| | | domestic % | unskilled % | supervisory % | trade % | artisans* % | w'collar % | misc.† % |
| Northern Province (*Bemba*) | Bemba | 7.56 | 46.20 | 9.04 | 0.90 | 25.48 | 4.45 | 6.37 |
| | Aushi | 17.96 | 43.93 | 5.10 | 0.88 | 18.83 | 5.28 | 8.02 |
| | Lunda (Kazembe) | 15.86 | 43.66 | 5.97 | 2.34 | 24.46 | 3.76 | 3.95 |
| Eastern Province (*Ngoni*) | Ngoni | 30.86 | 23.84 | 9.09 | 0.08 | 21.92 | 5.02 | 9.19 |
| | Cewa | 22.68 | 31.88 | 9.31 | 1.86 | 23.53 | 4.17 | 6.57 |
| | Nsenga | 19.29 | 44.01 | 8.49 | 0.89 | 16.35 | 3.88 | 7.09 |
| Central Province (*Lamba*) | Lamba | 35.27 | 39.73 | 3.12 | 0.40 | 11.50 | 2.50 | 7.48 |
| | Lala | 21.53 | 46.48 | 5.14 | 2.50 | 12.32 | 1.51 | 10.52 |
| Southern Province (*Barotse*) | Lozi | 5.98 | 54.20 | 17.47 | 1.62 | 6.80 | 10.19 | 3.74 |
| Western Province (*Lovale*) | Lovale | 1.66 | 73.66 | 8.08 | 0.83 | 11.32 | 1.13 | 3.32 |
| | Luchazi | — | 79.97 | 6.02 | — | 11.06 | 0.01 | 2.94 |
| | Chokwe | 1.03 | 75.12 | 3.91 | 1.03 | 16.96 | — | 1.95 |
| | Ndembu | 30.95 | 37.15 | 4.59 | 4.25 | 16.39 | 1.35 | 5.32 |
| Nyasaland | Tumbuka | 5.95 | 42.93 | 7.41 | 1.72 | 18.28 | 13.28 | 10.43 |
| | Henga | — | 47.16 | 9.10 | — | 18.96 | 14.78 | 10.00 |
| | Tonga | 17.26 | 26.40 | 12.98 | 6.93 | 14.45 | 19.62 | 2.36 |
| Tanganyika | Nyakyusa | 0.29 | 81.86 | 3.71 | — | 13.56 | — | 0.58 |

*Under artisans I have included carpenters, builders, and the like. For convenience I have also listed here those whom Mitchell classes as 'other skilled' i.e., tailors, lorry drivers, machine 'boys' working underground, etc.

† Under this rubric I have brought together a number of categories included in Mitchell's raw data, but which, because of the small numbers involved, could be ignored for present purposes: unemployed, agricultural workers, those recorded as being at school or college, or serving with the Army.

(Source: Clyde Mitchell: *Copperbelt Social Survey 1950-3*)

interesting questions of detail, it is sufficient for present purposes to bring out the contrasts in the position of the various ethnic groups by focussing just on two categories: the unskilled (including here the domestics) and the white-collar workers.

What emerges very clearly then is that there is considerable variation between groups in the degree to which they are represented in occupations evaluated in terms of high or low prestige. Without wishing to explore in detail the reasons for this development, it may be said that the facts of history and geography have the main part in accounting for it. Since access to the better-paid jobs is bound up with schooling, the role of the missions has obviously been crucial here, since for many years education for Africans was provided only in mission schools. Thus the earlier establishment of a Free Church of Scotland in Nyasaland (now Malawi) gave local Africans a long educational headstart over their fellows in Northern Rhodesia, so that later on the Copperbelt they tended to hold, together with the Lozi, the senior posts then open to Africans. Within Northern Rhodesia itself, the missionary 'occupation' had proceeded unevenly. Entering the country from the south, Coillard opened the first station of the Paris Evangelical Society in Barotseland in 1885, and he quickly came to exert an important influence in Barotse affairs, not least in the field of education. The other main point of entry to the country was in the north-east, through Tanganyika (Tanzania) and Nyasaland, whence came the White Fathers, the London Missionary Society, and the Church of Scotland, all of them to establish an abiding presence in their chosen areas. Yet despite all this activity, a vast but thinly populated part of the country had been left untouched by the missionary pioneers. This included Lamba country and the peoples to the west, the Lovale and Ndembu, for example (see Rotberg 1965:75). Although mission stations were later to be developed in all of these areas, off the beaten track, it seems as though a pattern of development had been set, for they were to remain for long backward and neglected (see p.19).

Varying experience in different parts of the country, the particular circumstances obtaining there, and the different ways in which they thus came to be involved in the new urban economy, serve to explain how certain groups are now associated with occupations carrying higher prestige, and have come to be regarded as 'important' tribes. But, if we ignore for the moment the 'outsiders' such as the people from Malawi or the Nyakyusa from Tanzania, what is of particular interest is the way this contemporary perception of ranking tends to coincide with that other view of the ranking system based on former military reputation and political dominance. There is no suggestion of course that the present-day pattern of relations between ethnic groups can be directly related to an ideology inherited from the past. What I think one can point to is the element of continuity in the situation. This consists in the fact that certain groups have been able to transpose their dominance of pre-colonial days into dominance in the contemporary urban context. For while at first glance the continuing emphasis on a military tradition appears as a mere harking back to the past, closer inspection suggests that its importance is more as a link between past and present. For the groups in question their former military tradition provided them with an idiom or language in which to interpret, and thus to adapt to, the new conditions in the towns, possibly even equipping them with a sense of self-assurance that is always important in confronting new situations and solving novel problems. The Copperbelt quickly became an arena in which ethnic groups competed with one another for prizes that were defined not in traditional terms, but in terms of the goals and values of an urban society. On the other hand, to the extent that groups which had formerly enjoyed dominance were also more successful in gaining a place in the urban sun, their sense of tribal identity was likely to be reinforced together with the sense of past history around which that identity was built.

I have indicated how the development of a system of ethnic ranking tied to occupation was closely interwoven with the workings of the colonial system. The latter factor, I believe, also helps us to understand why certain groups, themselves lacking a record of military success in the past, are nowadays prepared to accord higher prestige to those who possessed it. In my previous essay I referred to the joking relationship that exists between Bemba and Ngoni, noting how this expresses the fact that they were great enemies in the past, foes worthy of each other's mettle. I then described an episode when an Ngoni man once publicly assaulted the Bemba Paramount Chief Chitimukulu on one of his visits to the Copperbelt, and knocked him to the ground. I attempted to explain these various events by showing that the joking relationship operated not only within the field of intra-African relations, but that it also had to be set in the context of the wider field of Black-White relations; only in this way could we hope to make sense of the public affront to the chief. On his various official visits to the Copperbelt Chitimukulu was regarded not simply as the chief of a particular tribe, but as an African chief, a representative of the interests of the African people in opposition to the Europeans. His public reception on this particular occasion reflected the Africans' dissatisfaction over his failure to fulfil that expectation. A similar kind of argument can be offered to explain the general acceptance of former military reputation in contemporary ethnic ranking. The effect of colonialism in this part of Central Africa, as I have previously argued, was to introduce the African people to new relationships of dependence; in the new scheme of things theirs was a subordinate status, often carrying indeed a denial of their very manhood, as is evident, for example, in the way Africans of any age were commonly addressed or designated by Europeans as 'boy'.[6] In this context, I suggest, military prowess in the past similarly comes to be seen not simply as an attribute of particular groups such as the Bemba or the Ngoni, but of Africans as a whole. Their continuing recognition of martial reputation thus appears as a reassertion of manhood, in all the surrounding circumstances a peculiarly appropriate instrument for restoring the sense of pride in self and dignity.

The analysis I have just presented prompts a number of questions which I am not in a position to deal with adequately. What follows, therefore, are a few comments, derived from my earlier observations, pointing up areas for further enquiry. To begin with, it might seem that since the pattern of ethnic relations which I have just been describing for the Copperbelt was so rooted in the colonial situation, the achievement of political independence by Zambia would at once have initiated great changes in this regard. The first question then touches upon the future of ethnicity in the circumstances of new nationhood. A second, and closely related question, concerns the way the emergence of a middle-class elite bears on the expression of ethnic identity. Since the beginnings of such a class were already to be seen in the colonial period, it is convenient to start with the second issue.

It will be recalled from my earlier essay how, already during the fifties, there were a number of individuals who, holding some of the better-paid jobs then available to Africans, were beginning to develop an image of themselves as Africans rather than as members of a particular ethnic group. I cited as the example of such a person the case of a man I called Mulenga. Mulenga belonged to the relatively small number of those forming the new Copperbelt African elite; what we have also seen now is that this elite drew its membership preponderantly from a limited number of ethnic groups. Mulenga could thus confine his personal friendships to those of his own social class and still find that they mostly belonged to his own ethnic group. What appears to happen in such cases is that, by a kind of paradox, members of an advantaged ethnic group, secure in their own sense of social dominance, come to identify their own interests with those of the nation or state; their sense of ethnic identity is not extinguished, but is rather submerged within the wider identity. In the Zambian context, moreover, this development was also in tune with the needs of the day, for in the struggle towards national independence unity was the paramount consideration, to the achievement of which 'tribalism' was seen as a major obstacle. Yet, as we have also seen, ambiguity and contradiction were always there, and the cleavages within the elite frequently followed ethnic lines. The playing down of his ethnic identity was plainly much easier for the Bemba Mulenga than it was for the Lunda Mkamba who saw himself as still bound to his disadvantaged fellows from the far west of the country.

It is not difficult to see how these competitive relations between ethnic groups come to be carried on into the post-independence period. Indeed, independence must have intensified the competition. For new nationhood brought the promise of new prizes, not only in the shape of posts within the government itself or senior positions within the bureaucracy, but also by creating opportunities for new jobs and careers in the service of the state as well as in industry and commerce. As against this it seems clear, as a result of the earlier developments I have described, that not all groups would come to the starting-point equally endowed. One would expect, that is to say, that people from some parts of the country would be seriously handicapped, while others would confront the new situation from a position of entrenched advantage, which presumably they would seek to exploit further. In these circumstances there is likely to be a heightening of the sense of ethnic awareness among hitherto dominant groups and their satellites, as well as among the disadvantaged, with competition shifting increasingly to the national political arena.[7]

Because contradictory processes are at work, the situation is complex, bringing many personal dilemmas in its wake. One can imagine that many members of the elite are genuinely concerned to help in the development of a new national identity. Moreover, because 'tribalism' is likely to be a sensitive issue, and because they will be anxious to legitimize their dominant status, they can be expected to display a low ethnic profile. On the other hand, the very position of advantage they enjoy only serves to emphasize in the eyes of others the fact that social differentiation and distinction still coincide with ethnic divisions, and this in turn strengthens the system of ethnic categories that had developed in earlier days. Since these categories also tend to coincide with the main regions and provinces of the country, the major cleavages within the national social structure thus come to be perceived in ethnic terms. Such social pressures, interacting with the psychological processes at work in identity formation, combine to give new meaning to the sense of ethnic identity, and so presumably to the elements around which it is built. I have mentioned earlier how for certain groups their tribal history provided a link of continuity between their military dominance in the past and the status they were seeking to achieve for themselves in the new urban world. What then becomes of that tribal history when the dominance achieved in the colonial period is carried through into the days of independence? I am struck by the fact that some of the first major studies of local history by professional historians to be published recently are of such groups as the Bemba and Lozi (Roberts 1974; Caplan 1970). In such ways, one surmises, will the tradition of particular groups come to be woven into the fabric of national history and come to provide the new nation with some of its dominant symbols.

# 3. IDENTIFICATION WITH THE GRANDPARENTS AND ETHNIC IDENTITY

'The lost world would come back to him at many times, and often for no cause that he could trace or fathom — a voice half-heard, a word far-spoken, a leaf, a light that came and passed and came again. But always when that lost world would come back, it came at once, like a sound-thrust through the entrails, in all its panoply of past time, living, whole, and magic as it had always been.'

Thomas Wolfe: *Of Time and the River* (1935:200)

'Men may change their clothes, their wives, their religion, their philosophies, to a greater or lesser extent: they cannot change their grandfathers.'

Horace Kallen (cited in Gordon 1964:145)

In his book *Listening with the Third Ear*, in which he reflects on the inner experience of a psychoanalyst, Theodor Reik (1948:62-7) touches at one point on the problem of certain Jews who are ashamed of the fact that they are Jews. This leads him to embark on a lengthy digression in which he discourses on his own sense of ethnic identity. For a long time, he tells us, he had conceived of his people as an extension of his family and believed that his attitude towards them was similar to that which he had towards his own family. More than this, he believed that the attitude of any Jew must have its roots in his feelings towards his own family.

He then goes on:

'By this admittedly very personal concept of one's people as an extension of one's family I am attempting to explain to myself emotional facts that, often elusive in character, are hard to comprehend. This concept ... explained to me how one can feel more attracted to strangers and more hostile or critical towards one's own family. A man can prefer to be together with others and even avoid his own people; he can feel estranged from them — but he can never be a stranger to them. The very intimacy of the experience, which is nothing but common memories that have become unconscious, excludes the possibility of cutting a tie that was formed, not alone by the same blood, but by the same rhythm of living. It is neither congeniality nor consanguinity that speaks here, but the common destiny of our ancestors, of ourselves, and of our children, which forms a bond stronger than relations of another kind ... My people — these are the features and the faces of my parents, my brothers and sisters, my grandparents, my uncles and aunts, no longer recognised as such. I look into faces that have a family resemblance although they do not belong to my family, but to my people. They are perhaps not always sympathetic, these faces, but they are always "familiar" to me. I am an infidel Jew; I can scarcely read Hebrew any longer; I have only a smattering of Jewish history, literature and religion. Yet I know that I am a Jew in every fibre of my personality. It is as silly and as useless to emphasize as it is to disavow it. The only possible attitude toward it is to acknowledge it as a fact.'

Later, Reik goes on to note that, psychologically, being ashamed of one's parents is not identical with being ashamed of one's people. The latter is the expression of a tendency to deny the most essential part of oneself:

'... the best and most precious part we get from our parents, their parents and their ancestors, who continue to live in us ... The one feeling concerns only the personal shortcomings of an individual who was striving, sometimes succeeding and often failing. The other shame concerns something superpersonal, something beyond the narrow realm of the individual. It concerns the community of fate, it touches the bond that ties one generation to those preceding it and those following it.'

In these passages Reik introduces a number of themes which I have alluded to from time to time in the previous essays. In his account Reik presents himself as a man who, despite the fact that he has strayed far from the paths of traditional observance, has yet retained a profound sense of attachment to his ethnic group. There are other Jews, however, who are clearly less secure in their ethnic identity; some, as we have seen, find in it a conscious or unconscious sense of shame, while others seek to 'deny' it or even voluntarily to renounce it. There can be no simple answer in seeking to account for these differences in response, but Reik's comments are valuable in focussing attention on one element that appears to warrant closer examination: the nature and process of infantile attachments and identifications.

Reik himself was not seeking on this occasion to explore systematically the theoretical problem, but it is interesting to note that in one passage of his account he singles out the father as being of especial importance in the development of ethnic attitudes. Reik's relations with his father appear to have been very close, but it is also evident from some of his other writings that his mother's father was another very important attachment figure in his early childhood. After the death of his wife the grandfather, an orthodox Jew of great piety, came to live with the Reiks, and we learn that it was through being in the company of his grandfather around the house, in accompanying him on walks in the parks of Vienna, and in attending with him services in the synagogue that young Reik, then about five years old, acquired his knowledge of Jewish religion and ritual. Of his grandfather Reik (1964:53) himself records briefly: 'I was a little boy then and must have liked him very much at first. Later on, I hated him passionately because he was in permanent conflict with my father, his son-in-law. Grandfather was a religious fanatic and my father, whose part I took, an agnostic.' In spite of this the old man seems to have left a profound and lasting impression on the lad, for it is apparent from much of his writing that Reik retained throughout his life an abiding fascination with Jewish ritual. Only such a fascination can satisfactorily explain why Reik, approaching the end of his days, should devote himself to a book on the theme of pagan rites in Judaism. In this volume, far from appearing as a man unlearned in matters Jewish, he reveals himself in a sense as a talmudic scholar manqué. It would seem indeed as though the interest aroused in the Jewish religion in childhood could only be allowed expression in the adult Reik by being ground through the mill of psychoanalytic speculation and interpretation; as though, in other words, his book represented a compromise solution to the underlying and persisting conflict of identification with his father and grandfather.[1] But my purpose here is not to analyze the relations of Reik with his father and grandfather; it is rather to suggest that the relationship with the grandparents has rarely been given adequate attention in the psychoanalytic literature, and that moreover it can be of crucial importance in the formation of ethnic identity.

For the psychoanalysts of the classical era, busily engaged in laying the methodological foundations of the discipline, the grandparents emerge as shadowy figures lacking in substance and with little significance in the development of the child; they merited little theoretical attention. Ferenczi (1913), for example, could introduce his own brief note on the subject with the comment that the papers by Abraham and Jones, which had appeared a little earlier in the same journal, gave 'an almost exhaustive account of the significance that their relationships to the grandparents often assume for the whole life of the grandchildren'. Abraham's (1913) paper, itself only a few pages long, drew attention to the way many of his patients would constantly return to speaking of their grandparents or grandmother. Yet in none of these cases did the grandparents exercise a decisive influence upon the course of the patient's life. These cases, Abraham tells us, led invariably to one uniform conclusion: the special emphasis given to the grandfather or grandmother was always rooted in a violent rejection of the father or mother. Jones (1913a) treats the issue in rather greater detail, but the standpoint is essentially the same. According to Jones, the interest, the admiration, and the fantasies that gather round the figure of the grandfather are always derived from an attitude of mind taken up earlier in respect to the father. Both here and in a later article on the fantasy of the reversal of generations (1913b) Jones points to the grandchild's wish to identify himself with the grandparent. Thus he refers to a belief of children that 'as they grow older their relative position to their parents will be gradually reversed, so that finally they will become the parents, and their parents the children'. As a result of this fantasy the child is in imagination the actual parent of its parents, that is, equivalent to its own grandparents. 'We doubtless have here', Jones (1913b:677) claims, 'the deepest reason for the constant identification of grandson with grandfather; both are equally feared by the father, who has reason to dread their retaliation for his guilty wishes against them'. Such a view is a pointer to, as well as consistent with, the broader generalization with which he concludes that 'all members of the family group, from brother to grandfather, from sister to aunt, are all replacement-formations of the image of the original trinity of father, mother and child' (Jones 1913a:673).[2]

Jones's argument here seems to me to be somewhat confused for the identification he is seeking to explain is presented from the point of view of the father, not from the perspective of the grandchild, which is the point at issue. But to the anthropologist the most striking feature of this discussion is the scant regard that is paid to social reality. Ferenczi does observe that whether the image of the 'feeble grandfather' or the 'powerful grandfather' becomes a fixation for the child depends on the part that the grandfather really plays in the family, while Jones also observes how the identification is often furthered through the greater tenderness and forbearance that commonly marks the attitude of an older man towards children. On the other hand, to treat the grandparents simply as a substitute or surrogate for the parents is to deny them their own distinctive social role, and hence a psychological reality in their own right.[3] Such a view of the grandparents, if it does not actually derive from, is at least congruent with the classical model of the oedipal situation, a model that in turn, as has frequently been noted, reflects a form of family organization that had come to prevail among the Viennese middle class of the day. It was in this way, for example, that Freud (1909:237) could say that 'for the small child his parents are at first the only authority and the source of all belief', an assumption which elsewhere finds more technical expression in the concept of the super-ego as a precipitate or representation of the child's early relations to his parents. Such a conception seems now not only to be unnecessarily ethnocentric, it also misses a point that was to be emphasized later by Flügel (1948: 163) that 'the tendency of the child to imitate the grandparent may constitute an important factor in moulding the child's beliefs, attitudes, desires and occupations'.

The significance of the grandparents in this regard emerges immediately when we turn to ethnographic accounts of other, non-western, societies. To cite but two examples: among the Swazi of South Africa the grandparents are said to 'teach the young to respect their parents'. As Kuper (1950:105) reports:

'Grandparents "scold by the mouth", parents more often "with the stick". The law of the past issues in the voice of the grandfather, and he must give his sanction and opinion on any important event, such as the marriage of a grandchild. The power exercised by apparently decrepit ancients over sons and grandsons is partly explained by the fact that they are "nearest to the ancestors" and essential officiators in all domestic rituals. The grandmother — *ugogo* — is the main teacher of the young. She sees that the correct ritual is performed to ensure the health and proper development of the grandchildren and she supervises the numerous ceremonies which punctuate their growth in status. In many districts a woman, after she has borne a child, is not allowed into the great hut until the baby can crawl, when it is laid to the supporting poles of the hut and then into the courtyard where the granny is waiting; she puts a little ash from the hearth on its forehead so that "it will be one with its forefathers". When the grandchildren are weaned they are usually put in her charge, and they sleep with her till approaching puberty, when boys and girls move to separate quarters.'

Swazi society is marked by a strong emphasis on the agnatic principle, but the distinctive role of the grandparents is no less pronounced in matrilineal societies. Thus Fortes (1950:276) tells us that among the Ashanti of Ghana the grandparents on both sides are the most honoured of all one's kinsfolk; they are the prototypes of persons and institutions commanding reverence and submission to the norms of tradition. The maternal grandmother holds a position of particular importance. By custom, birth should take place in the mother's home, so that the children often spend their earliest years at the place of the maternal grandparents. And although care of the young child falls chiefly on the mother, the grandmother too plays a significant part in its rearing. Indeed, Fortes notes (1950:263) that grandmothers can sometimes be very autocratic in this regard, arguing that a grandchild belongs more to the lineage than to its parents and therefore comes more appropriately under its grandmother's care. But the child also enjoys a special relationship with all its grandparents:

'Grandparents lavish affection on their grandchildren, who are their greatest pride. Grandparents can reprimand and punish their grandchildren for minor acts of disobedience or impropriety. In cases of serious misdemeanour they must call on the parents to take disciplinary action. It is from the grandparents of both sexes that children learn family history, folk-lore, proverbs and other traditional lore. The grandparents are felt to be living links with the past. They are looked up to with reverence, not only as the repositories of ancient wisdom but also as symbols of continuity of descent.'

These and similar observations in African societies and elsewhere have been brought together and synthesized in a couple of important contributions by Radcliffe-Brown. His first treatment of the issue was in the context of a discussion of 'joking relationships'. He noted (1952:96-7) that in many societies there was what anthropologists have come to speak of as a joking relationship between relatives of alternate generations. The joking in this instance is of a relatively mild kind: grandchildren make fun of their grandparents and of those who are called grandfather and grandmother in accordance with the classificatory system of terminology, and these reply in kind. A joking relationship, in Radcliffe-Brown's view, always includes elements of incompatibility. So, in this case, while grandparents and grandchildren are united by kinship, they are also separated by age and by the social difference that results from the fact that as the grandchildren are in the process of entering into full participation in the social life of the community the grandparents are gradually retiring from it. Important duties towards his relatives in his own and even more in his parents' generation, Radcliffe-Brown points out, impose upon an individual many restraints; but with those of the second ascending generation there can be, and usually is, a relationship of simple friendliness relatively free from restraint. Whereas, that is to say, the relationship between parent and child is generally marked by dominance on the one hand and subordination on the other, that of grandparent and grandchild frequently takes the form of an 'alliance' of alternate generations.

Although this kind of institutionalized joking relationship is fairly widespread, it is by no means universal. Apple (1956) has suggested that its presence or absence is to be related to other features of family social structure, in particular the extent to which the grandparents are themselves figures of authority or are dissociated from it. Nevertheless, what should be plain is that Radcliffe-Brown was not offering a psychological analysis, as Apple asserts, but a social structural one. Parents and grandparents always occupy differentiated roles *vis-à-vis* child and grandchild, and this is linked with the fact, as he puts it in his Introduction to *African Systems of Kinship and Marriage*, that one generation is replaced in course of time by the generation of the grandchildren. That the two generations are regarded as being in a relation, not of superordination and subordination, but of simple friendliness and solidarity and something approaching social equality is merely an expression of the same structural principle (Radcliffe-Brown 1950:28-9).

Radcliffe-Brown, like the other anthropologists on whose data Apple relied, was of course concerned here with societies of a type in which kinship was of crucial importance in the social structure, and where social groups and their interrelations were frequently defined and regulated in terms of kinship principles. In what way, then, can these ideas have relevance in a modern or modernizing society, in particular to the role of ethnicity within it? It is important to repeat here that Radcliffe-Brown's was a sociological analysis. In adopting a structural approach his discussion of the grandparent-grandchild relationship was built up around, and sought to explain, certain modes of social behaviour of a regular and recurring kind. Thus he confines his attention to such matters as the custom of permitted disrespect that grandchildren display towards their grandparents in certain societies or how through the terminological merging of alternate generations certain social divisions within a society may be brought into being. Such customs or social arrangements point to a structural identification of alternate generations, but they may also be said to pre-suppose, or at least to be accompanied by, a process of identification in the psychological sense. The psychological process is a much more complex, subtle, and flexible one than the sociological; it depends not so much on formal, prescribed modes of behaviour, but much more on the way a particular relationship has actually been experienced, directly or indirectly, interpreted or woven into fantasy. To a considerable extent, indeed, identification in this sense proceeds at the level of the unconscious so that its later conscious expression is often built upon a residue of infantile memories and associations; the admired traits of the love object have, to use Jacobson's (1964:51) phrase, become enduringly introjected into the child's wishful self images. It should also be added, perhaps, that such identification with another is rarely, if ever, total and complete; the task of building up an ego-identity consists in piecing together the various partial identifications of one's childhood — what Erikson calls identity fragments — into some kind of coherent whole. Radcliffe-Brown was not, of course, concerned with such issues, but his structural analysis nonetheless does suggest, I think, an approach to the problem of the role that grandparents can play in identification and identity in a modern polyethnic situation.

It has commonly been observed of such situations created by migration how the second generation frequently rebels against the authority of the parents, in particular the father, and quickly comes to reject the traditional way of life and the values to which the parents remained committed. The point is well summed up in the remarks of a son about his father recorded by Warner and Srole (1945:152):

'Oh, he gets me sick ... At every little thing I do, he preaches at me. Not that he forbids me to do it, mind you. He has more sense than that. But simply he's always telling me how they used to do things in Russia. Well, that's all very interesting, but this happens to be the United States of America not Russia, and the twentieth century, not the nineteenth ... He thinks I don't respect him. Well, he's right, and you can see my reasons.'

In the changed circumstances obtaining in the host society, instead of looking to the parents for the pattern and content of his social personality, we are told, the child cuts himself off from his parents' orientating efforts and takes his 'design for living' from models outside the home. 'Altogether, the generations become estranged and isolated from each other.' It was this development that underlay Warner's and Srole's model of assimilation with its assumption of the more or less rapid demise of ethnic groups. Yet, as we have seen, the expectations of that model have not been borne out. On the contrary, in the third and fourth generations we even come to hear of 'ethnic resurgence'. This does not take the form of an attempt to revive a way of life that has gone so much as an increasing concern with ethnic identity and a search for means of giving it expression in changed social circumstances. The issue is a complex one which allows no easy answers. All I wish to suggest here is that in approaching it in the past insufficient attention has been paid to the nature of the relationship with the grandparents.

My hypothesis can be stated fairly simply. Where, within the structure of the family, authority vests in the parents, and especially the father, we can expect tensions to arise of the typical oedipal kind. These tensions mount as the child approaches adolescence and enters early adulthood, leading to bitter conflicts between adjacent generations and, in a polyethnic situation, to increased questioning, even rejection, of the parents and the values they represent. In this second generation the sense of attachment to the ethnic group is thus likely to be impaired. But where in the succeeding generation there has been a warm and indulgent relation with the grandparents of the kind so often described by anthropologists for non-western societies the opposition between adjacent relations is counteracted by the identification that develops between alternate generations. It is in this process of identification with the grandparents that the child comes to associate himself with certain of the values to which they subscribe, and it is in this way that the grandparents come to serve as a symbol of continuity, offering an anchor for the sense of ethnic identity. Needless to say, I am not attempting here to set up the grandparents at the expense of the parents; my point rather is to draw attention to the complementary roles that they play. Nor am I asserting that the relationship with the grandparents is always, or necessarily, warm, indulgent, and protective, or that it invariably leads to the consequences I have postulated. Like other human relationships, that with the grandparents can be complex and many-sided; its character is shaped not only by prescribed and formal rules of behaviour, but no less by questions of temperament and social circumstance, and of the wider structure of relationships within which it is embedded so that the nature of the relationship in each instance has to be established empirically. What the hypothesis does claim is that the relationship with the grandparents is likely to present a marked contrast to that with the parents. Furthermore, where the grandparents are accessible and responsive — to use Bowlby's (1973) terms — they are apt to be ideally suited to play the part of attachment figures. In these circumstances the relationship is likely to be conducive to the development of a positive ethnic identity.

Allowing for the qualifications, what is the evidence in support of this view? In terms of my own present knowledge, the answer is: scarcely any. Because of their theoretical assumptions, as I have already noted, psychoanalysts have displayed little interest in extra-familial kinship; according to Rappaport (1958:518), in his effort to retrace symptoms and character traits, the analyst will usually probe his patient's relations with the parents, but 'inquiry stops short of the grandparents'.[4] Nor, as it happens, are the anthropologists very much more helpful. Some years ago Firth (1956:11) was able to remark that in British society problems of the structure and function of *kinship*, as distinct from the structure and function of the *elementary family*, had received little attention as yet; and in America the position appears to have been much the same. More recently a number of valuable studies have been carried out on both sides of the Atlantic (e.g. Firth, Hubert, and Forge 1969; Schneider 1968); even so they offer little information on the issue with which I am presently concerned. In these circumstances I have thought it best to present a few illustrations from Jewish culture and experience which I have culled rather arbitrarily from a variety of sources; these are intended not so much to confirm the hypothesis as to serve as pointers to a more general problem that merits, I believe, more systematic investigation.

Many observers have drawn attention to the importance that kinship plays in Jewish life. Jewishness, it is said, is often experienced as a feeling of family loyalty, a strong attachment to *mishpocha* — a concept that can include a variable range of relatives. As Berman (1968:236, 309) puts it, kinship feeling lies at the heart of the Jewish ethos, and Jewish identity may run very deep in a person for whom religious ritual is far less important than a feeling of belonging to an extended Jewish family. At the centre of this ring of kin of course are the parents. Embedded in the very roots of Jewish thought is the notion of obligation, and among the earliest duties the child learns to acquire is that of the obedience and respect owed to the parents. In the *shtetl*, Zborowski and Herzog (1952:295) tell us, no commandment claimed more vivid adherence — to the letter and to the spirit — than the ancient injunction to 'honour thy Father and thy Mother'. But while the mother is usually presented as a devoted and indulgent figure, the father often appears as more forbidding, at once remote and less demonstrative in his affection. Respect for the father was often mingled with fear, though it has been noted that fear here carries the meaning of awe rather than of fright (1952:296). The father displayed a keen interest in the child's development, particularly in the field of learning, but from the perspective of the child he remained essentially a figure of authority. Though not averse on occasion to the use of physical punishment, more often it was through fear of the 'look' that he maintained discipline. Although the mother played a more protective role she too played a part in disciplining the child so that both parents at times tended to merge in a single composite persona, as evidenced in the Yiddish expression the *tateh-mammah*, a recognition of the unity of the parents. In these circumstances it was often the grandparents to whom the child turned for solace.

Recognition of the contrasting roles of parents and grandparents, in particular of father and grandfather, is to be found at once in the *brith*, the rite of circumcision performed on the eighth day after birth by which male offspring are introduced to the Covenant. In the ancient tradition it was the father himself who performed the operation, but for countless generations, at least in Europe, the act has been carried out by a ritual specialist or *mohel*, and the father's role has been confined to offering the solemn prayer of dedication in which he recites the major obligations that are entailed in entry into the Covenant. The other major part in the rite, at least since the ninth or tenth century in Europe, is taken by the *sandek*[5] whose task it is to receive the child, usually from the grandmother. Then, seated in, or next to, the chair of the Prophet Elijah, held to be present on these occasions as the Guardian Angel, the *sandek* holds the child while the operation is performed, giving him comfort. The *sandek* should be a pious, God-fearing man; if still alive, he is usually the paternal grandfather. (Incidentally, it is in the course of the *brith* that the child's name is first publicly pronounced. In Jewish law the child is always named with reference to the father — i.e. son or daughter of — but the personal name will recall a relative already dead, usually one of the grandparents. Through the name, therefore, the individual is normally linked immediately with the two preceding generations.)

Thus the *brith* serves as a kind of model for the child's developing relations with parents and grandparents. In the recital of the blessing on this occasion the first obligation that the father undertakes is to dedicate his son to Torah, to the study of the Law. And, until the lad reaches the age of ritual maturity, the father should encourage the child to study and, indeed, should also adopt the role of teacher. However, the grandfather too has an important role here and, given the tension in the father-son relationship, we are not surprised to discover that it is the grandfather from whom the child acquires much of his learning. We have seen an instance of this in the case of Theodor Reik mentioned earlier, but it is far from unique. In the lines of dedication with which he opens his book of tales about the Hassidim, the novelist Elie Wiesel (1972) expresses movingly the contrasting roles played by father and grandfather in his own development:

'My father, an enlightened spirit, believed
in man.
My grandfather, a fervent Hasid, believed
in God.
The one taught me to speak, the other to sing.
Both loved stories.
And when I tell mine, I hear their voices.
Whispering from beyond the silent storm,
they are what links the survivor to their memory.'

I take one final illustration of the point from the pen of Moses Hess which, because of its contemporary ring, has particular relevance to the present discussion. Born in 1812, Hess was very much a product of the Enlightenment, deeply influenced by the intellectual and ideological currents that were coming to swirl in the capitals of Europe as he entered his young manhood. Soon he had moved far from the orthodox Judaism in which he had been reared, for, as he recorded once in his personal diary at the time, the Jewish religion, as such, had died out. 'Mosaic law can neither bind the Jews together, nor satisfy their religious needs.' (Cited in Litvinoff 1965:19). Marrying a non-Jewish wife, Hess began to emerge as a significant figure in the European socialist movement of the day. At one time a friend and collaborator of Karl Marx, one of those indeed who had done most to bring Marx to socialism (Wolfe 1965: 244), he and Marx later parted company. Then at some stage he appears to have had what can fairly be described as a conversion experience, in this instance more accurately perhaps one of reconversion, and with the publication in 1862 of his book *Rome and Jerusalem* (Eng.tr. 1918) his was to become a major voice of a renascent Jewish nationalism — some might even claim its inventor (see Berlin 1959). In this book he rails not only against his German Jewish brethren who were seeking in assimilation a solution to 'the Jewish problem', but no less against the 'reformers of its religion' who had 'sucked the marrow out of Judaism', leaving nothing to remain 'but the shadow of a skeleton'. And he asks what would have happened to the people if they had not, through the institutions of the Talmudic sages, thrown a protecting fence around their religion, so as to safeguard it for the coming days. At one point (p. 87) he recalls the words of his mother, who died when he was fourteen:

'Listen, my child, you must study diligently. Mohrich [a celebrated Talmudic scholar] was one of my ancestors, and you are fortunate that you are studying under your grandfather. It is written that "when grandfather and granchild study the Torah together, the study of the divine law will never forsake the family, but will be handed down from generation to generation."'

Later, Hess speaks of the grandfather himself:

'This confidence and joy remind me vividly of my grandfather ... My grandfather was neither a poet nor a prophet; he was only a plain businessman, who in the daytime attended to his routine work, and in the night devoted himself to religion and scholarly studies.'

The nature of the bond between them, and the affective source of many of Hess's later ideas, emerge more clearly as he recalls episodes from their times together: how, for example, his grandfather wept as he read to him Jeremiah's vision of Rachel, in her tomb in Ramah, lamenting over her children as they were carried off before her eyes to the Babylonian captivity, or when he showed him olives and dates, saying with shining eyes, 'These come from Eretz Yisroel'.

Studying with the grandfather is of course only one of the many ways in which his image can be stamped upon the memory of a child, laying down a model for the later conduct of his life, at least in some of its aspects. Some relate to formal contexts, others to informal ones arising out of the casual interactions of daily life. Among the formal contexts I include here those occasions when people assemble for a ritual or ceremony. Anthropologists have long recognized the importance these gatherings have for promoting sentiments of solidarity. What is so notable about Jewish observance in this respect is that so many of them are, as Sklare and Greenblum put it, child-centred, and a rich source therefore for building up memories and associations. Sklare and Greenblum (1967:68-70) make the interesting observation that in a community like Lakeville, where ritual observance has declined to minimal levels, childhood memories reinforce the influence of the parental example, and have a positive effect on present levels of observance. Of all the festivals recalled in this way by their respondents the service of the Seder, celebrating the Passover, was cited most frequently. The Seder ceremony is of especial interest to my present concerns because its central and explicit purpose is to communicate to the children, and have them re-live as it were the nuclear experience of the Jewish people — the Exodus from Egypt. Of the Seder, Maurice Samuel (1948:130) has written with feeling and insight:

> 'There is no way of comparing the hold of the Seder on a Jewish child's memory with that of Christmas on a Christian child's; and the attempt would be tasteless, as well as pointless. But let it be said that the Seder ceremony has been specially devised by generations of pedagogues to appeal to children. Its ritual is charming, ingenious and powerful ... The child who has sat through a few Seders carries into later years an unforgettable Passover nostalgia.'

What also needs to be noted here is that traditionally, while they are alive, the Seder is held at the home of one or other of the pair of grandparents. Normally the father is the head of his own household, and it is he who conducts the regular domestic rituals such as the weekly sanctification to greet the Sabbath. The Seder, however, is an occasion for the gathering of the whole 'family', and it is the grandfather who officiates.

Ceremonies of this kind achieve much of their impact not only because of the sense of intimacy they generate, but also because they occur infrequently; they provide a dramatic way of introducing a temporal order into human affairs. Many childhood memories, however, are of a more mundane, though no less powerful, character, built out of more fleeting impressions and personal experiences. Without deliberate study such processes are difficult to document, and I will content myself here with a single illustration taken from a short story 'Defender of the Faith' by the American novelist Philip Roth (1959). The story, set in the weeks following the end of the last war in Europe, has as its central character Nathan Marx, a Sergeant in the US Army. Marx is a seasoned and efficient soldier for whom the fact that he is Jewish has almost become an irrelevance until it is revived by a private, a fellow Jew and a malingerer, who seeks to exploit Marx's Jewishness for his own advantage. Roth's story is concerned with the conflict set off in this way in the soldier's mind, but in the telling a key element is the description of Marx's re-awakening to his ethnic identity. '... But now one night-noise, one rumour of home and time past, and memory played down through all I had anaesthetized, and came to what I suddenly remembered was myself.' (p. 184)

A little later his memory is stirred again on hearing the use of the word *leben*, a term of endearment, 'my grandmother's word for me'. This is followed by a more specific association:

'Out of the many recollections of my childhood that had tumbled over me these past few days I heard my grandmother's voice: "What are you making a *tsimmes?*" It was what she would ask my mother when, say, I had cut myself while doing something I shouldn't have done, and her daughter was bawling me out. I needed a hug and a kiss and my mother would moralize. But my grandmother knew — mercy overrides justice. I should have known it too. Who was Nathan Marx to be such a penny pincher with kindness?' (p. 207)

My discussion so far has been predicated on the assumption, fully met in all the examples I have cited, that grandchildren have easy and regular access to the grandparents and that contiguity makes for the development of a meaningful relationship between them. In the past this was certainly so. Judaism is essentially a religion of community. Other factors aside, the fact, for example, that many central observances require the presence of a quorum of adult males, the *minyan*, or the dependence on a variety of ritual specialists who can only be supported by a congregation, helped to ensure that wherever Jews moved they at once established local communities with their own communal institutions. We have seen earlier how this pattern was maintained throughout the long process of Jewish settlement in America, and we have seen too how the Jews of Eastern European origin continued to live out an encapsulated existence within the ghettos and even in the areas of secondary settlement. But what happens when, with continuing upward social mobility, the move takes place, as I have previously described, from the 'gilded ghettos' to the suburbs or even to another part of the country? In their study of Lakeville Sklare and Greenblum excluded consideration of the grandparents from their enquiries. A notable finding of their study, however, concerns the changing pattern of personal interaction: there was a marked shift from the family to the friendship circle.[6] The inference one draws from this is that the relationship with the grandparents must be seriously affected, contact in some cases becoming minimal, in others perhaps even eliminated. What are the consequences of this? In terms of the argument I have been seeking to develop, one would expect to find that among young people of the fourth generation, brought up in the comfortable affluence of the suburbs, many would experience a particularly severe crisis of identity. For in the absence of an intimate relationship with the grandparents, with whom they can identify, there is little to counteract, and so cut across, the opposition and hostility towards the parents. There is rebellion, as in the past, but now the family system would appear to provide young people with few models which would serve to reintegrate them into the group. Here again, in the absence of systematic research, this must remain for the present no more than hypothesis. In troubled and changing times the experience of a generation is not uniform and, as Lipset and Raab (1970) have emphasized, ought not to be reduced to facile generalizations about the 'generation gap'. But what seems plain is that young Jews have been fully represented in all, or nearly all, the various movements that have attracted the youth of America in recent years, and that many of them have come in the process to cast off their ethnic identity. We are dealing here with a complex social phenomenon which is not satisfactorily to be accounted for in terms of some simple one-to-one correlation. I would like to suggest, however, that any study of these young people which omits consideration of the relationship with the grandparents may be missing an important factor in their situation.

In developing this analysis I have deliberately confined myself to examples drawn from Jewish life, but I do not consider the situation I have outlined to be a peculiarly Jewish phenomenon, though it may have its own distinctive cultural overtones. On the contrary, I believe that the principles to which I draw attention have a more general application. Freud (1909:237) has remarked that 'indeed, the whole progress of society rests upon the opposition between successive generations'. This may well be the case, but to adopt such a restricted view is to overlook the fact that continuity is no less a prerequisite of the survival and advance of society. Moreover, to focus analysis too narrowly on adjacent generations is to miss a point of crucial significance in the understanding of human kinship as a cultural institution. It is not too difficult perhaps to see the counterpart of the father in a society of non-human primates; on the other hand, in no animal society do we find recognition of the grandfather. In this sense the grandparents are the more distinctively human figures. Without them there can be no meaningful concept of collateral relationships, so that the grandparents become the essential focal points in the emergence and binding together of groups which mark the beginnings of human society. It is the grandparents moreover who provide the necessary links between the generations, past and present. They are the symbols of continuity, and it is no accident that in so many societies the term for grandparent is synonymous with that for ancestor, or that, as the repositories of traditional knowledge and values, they are so often indispensable to.the ritual life of the community. In her autobiography Margaret Mead (1972) has provided a revealing account of the importance of her grandmother in her own life. In a later chapter she writes on becoming a grandmother herself, remarking that in the presence of grandparents and grandchildren past and future merge in the present. She concludes with this comment: 'My friend Ralph Blum has defined the human unit of time as the space between a grandfather's memory and a grandson's knowledge of these as he has heard about them. We speak a great deal here about a human scale: we need also a human unit in which to think about time.'[7] Anthropologists in fact have come to recognize the necessity for such a unit of time in dealing with the vicissitudes of domestic groups (see, e.g. Goody 1958). There seems good reason to believe that such a perspective can be applied with equal profit to the understanding of ethnicity and ethnic identity.

# NOTES

## Chapter 1

1 Freud himself appears to have used the term only once in a more than casual way. This was in a reference to his own Jewish identity (see Erikson 1968:21).

2 For example, between 1950, when Clyde Mitchell began his social survey of the Copperbelt African population, and 1955, when I embarked on my study of Ndola, the number of Africans in Ndola had increased from about 20,000 to somewhere between 40-50,000.

3 In the earliest years mine officials found themselves puzzled when large numbers of their African labour force would suddenly decamp. Inquiry quickly established that the men had returned home for the annual tree-cutting and preparation of the new *citimene* gardens. But soon this practice was abandoned, and young migrants began to send small sums of money home so that others could be employed to do the seasonal work in their stead. Over the years considerable sums of money have continued to flow back to the villages in the form of remittances, a fact the significance of which has been discussed in detail by Godfrey Wilson (1940). However, so far as I am aware, the practice of sending money home specifically for tree-cutting ceased a long time ago.

4 Although commonly employed as a technical term in the anthropological literature, its value as a tool of analysis has frequently been questioned (see, e.g. Southall 1970). In addition to the objections that have been raised against it on heuristic grounds, it has also been much criticized recently on account of its implicit ideological assumptions (see, e.g. van den Berghe 1965; Apthorpe 1968). In this essay the words 'tribe' and 'tribalism' are used as folk categories, that is, terms commonly employed by English-speaking Africans. Where ChiBemba, now the *lingua franca* of the Copperbelt, and the only vernacular which I

myself acquired, is being used the words most commonly heard are *mutundu* or *mushobo*.

5 Mitchell's study of *Kalela* was carried out in Luanshya in 1951. My own researches, conducted chiefly at Luanshya and Ndola, spanned the years 1950-56. I have made no attempt here to update the material, so that the 'ethnographic present', unless the context plainly indicates otherwise, relates to this period only.

6 Literally, the 'six-o' clock people'. This is a reference to the time of sunset. The Lunda, Lovale, Cokwe, and Luchazi groups are thus linked together as people from the land of the setting sun. The expression implies contempt for a benighted people.

7 We have here another illustration of the way in which 'tribe' serves as a categorizing device. In this instance the term 'Kasai' is used as though it referred to a particular tribe in the Congo (now Zaire). In fact, no such group exists; 'Kasai' turns out simply to be a category term applied to all Africans on the Copperbelt who have come from the Congo. Conversely, the 'Kasai' referred to all Zambian Africans as Lamba, a group whose tribal territory adjoins, and in the past included, much of what is now the Copperbelt.

8 That matters may be more complex than this is well illustrated in an episode that occurred a short time before I began work in Ndola. Two Bisa factions had been in contention over the ownership and use of the *Kalela* drums. The tension mounted to the point where on one occasion an open brawl was only prevented by the intervention of the police. Thereafter two teams were formed, and they competed in a *Kalela* dance in which they expressed their mutual hostility by addressing their taunting verses at one another.

9 Stereotypes may also include positive evaluations, but these tend to be made within the context of the stereotype as a whole and thus serve to highlight the generally negative impression; they are the exceptions that prove the rule.

10 From this point of view Harries-Jones (cited in Mitchell 1970:96) may be correct that it is a mistake to adduce evidence of 'tribalism' from the existence of 'home-boy' cliques. Members of such cliques may not think of themselves primarily as fellow tribesmen. To outsiders, however, seeing them together, that is precisely how they are likely to appear. We have here an excellent example of the need not only to distinguish carefully the 'internal' and 'external' frames, but to note them in their interaction.

11 The importance that attached to having a formal constitution was a striking feature in all the attempts with which I was familiar to establish any new kind of voluntary association. It seemed at times, as in the formation of an African Drama Club in which I participated, that the drafting of the constitution was more important than the activities themselves for which the new group was being brought into being.

12 For many years the location authorities in Ndola had recognized certain Elders as representatives of the different ethnic groups making up the population of the location. Each Elder was given a badge of office, and

a number of them would gather in the evenings at *chitenge*, a 'shelter' adjoining the Location Superintendent's office, in order to hear minor disputes and complaints among the people. Many of the Elders also received people at their houses and sought to help them with their various problems. The mode of selection of Elders varied from one group to another. In some cases elections were conducted at a gathering of members of the tribe in question, in others the Elder acquired his position when, on a visit to town, a chief of the tribe named him as his 'representative' there. In fact, nearly every Elder claimed close relationship to his chief, and in town would take on that chief's name. A fuller account of the work and position of Tribal Elders in the municipal locations is given in Epstein (1958).

13 In the days when tribal representation still operated in the mine compounds, Elders enjoyed certain privileges, including a special ration allowance to enable them to take care of new arrivals and other visitors. This did not occur in the municipal locations so that the appointment of additional Elders posed no problems for the location officials.

14 Some tension developed between the two bodies over preparations for the reception of Chitimukulu on his 1952 visit. For reasons which will become evident in the later discussion, local Congress leaders were anxious to play the role of host on this occasion. The matter was quickly sorted out, and the two groups agreed to act in concert.

15 Coffins, otherwise a major item of expense, were frequently provided by the compound and location authorities.

16 The traditional greeting for a Bemba chief, still to be observed in the villages, requires that the subject throw himself on his back and clap his hands.

17 This is a reference to the *citimene* system of cultivation practised in many parts of rural Zambia. In Bemba country itself the trees are pollarded, the cut timber gathered together and burned, and the seed then planted in the ash-bed.

18 Joking relations between tribes on the Copperbelt have been well described by Mitchell (1956). In this particular instance the relationship is based on the fact that in pre-colonial times Bemba and Ngoni were great military enemies (see essay 2). One of the most important features of the relationship emerges at funerals: Bemba and Ngoni bury each other's dead, and as they do so they hurl taunts at their erstwhile foes. In the episode reported here, the joking relationship operated as a mechanism of social control, a point not hitherto documented for the Copperbelt, though familiar enough in the general ethnographic literature (see, e.g. Colson 1953; cf. Mitchell 1956:38).

19 The Lunda of Kawambwa are to be distinguished from the Lunda of the North-western Province referred to earlier. Although both groups claim to be offshoots of the great empire of Mwatayanvwa whose suzerainty once embraced a vast area of what is now Zaire, after their departure from the homeland they went their separate ways, and now differ in important respects in social organization and culture, including language. As we have seen, on the Copperbelt the Western Lunda are

associated, and associate themselves, with the peoples of the North-western Province. The Lunda of Kazembe, on the other hand, are associated with the Bemba with whom they share a basically similar culture and language.

20 *Bwanas:* a common term of reference and address for Europeans. Here it referred to senior members of the Kawambwa District staff, the District Commissioner and District Officer.

*Capricorn Chiti:* this was a reference to the Capricorn Society, an organization that had recently come into being with the stated aims of promoting the building up of a multi-racial society in Central Africa based on the partnership of Black and White. The initiative for the formation of the Society came from Southern Rhodesia, and many Africans in the north regarded it with intense suspicion. Those Africans who appeared to be wavering in their opposition to federation, whether or not they had actually joined the Society or even expressed sympathy with its aims, were promptly labelled 'Capricornists', people who had betrayed the African cause.

21 The expression used was *uwaifinya*, literally one who makes himself heavy or important.

22 It had been announced that on the Sunday afternoon Kazembe himself would dance. The crowd that day was even greater than before, so that at the last moment the venue had to be changed to one of the football pitches. At the football ground, however, the location police had diffi-culty in organizing the crowd, many of whom had come straight from the Beer Hall, and in the end the dance had to be cancelled. This aroused a good deal of resentment, but it was directed mainly at the local authorities, not at the chief himself.

23 This appears to be a reference to an incident that occurred shortly after the arrival of the party at the Government offices in Ndola. Recognizing that the chief would be feeling dirty after the long, dusty journey, the young District Officer pointed to a nearby water-tap where he could have a wash. The Africans were naturally affronted by this insult to the chief and Kazembe himself was said to have admonished the DO in very forthright terms. Later, on the journey to the location, Kazembe refused to allow himself to be driven by the DO. It appears too that because of threats of boycotts and strikes on the Copperbelt at that time, the arrangements for the visit had been upset so often that Kazembe had finally lost patience, and had insisted on going this time. The tour thus began without prior consultation with, or approval of, the Provincial Commissioner at Kasama who was said to have cabled his strong disapproval to Kawambwa.

24 It may be worth mentioning here that at Ndola the word *kalela* had come to refer to a pair of trousers which, while they looked smart, were really of inferior cut and quality, a point which neatly confirms Mitchell's analysis. I think the fact that the dress of the dancers is also exaggerated (e.g. the number of handkerchiefs or fountain-pens displayed in the breast-pocket) — a point that Mitchell does not stress — also assumes importance in this connection.

25 The establishment of Local Government Councils has of course given the village a degree of formal organization that it almost certainly did not possess in pre-contact times. One of the aims behind the introduction of the Councils was to move from the village to the 'area' as the local unit of administration (see Epstein 1969:255). Nevertheless, despite the important changes that this represented, the new system also allowed for some degree of continuity. For, since the Councillors represented villages, in some respects the Council merely provided a new arena to which pre-existing relations of competition could be transferred.

26 Tolai are inveterate chewers of the pepper-plant which is invariably taken together with the slaked lime-powder (*kabang*). The production of *kabang*, from coral collected on the reefs, is regularly undertaken by Matupi women, who also make the small packets (*vaum*) in which it is sold. *Kabang* is another important source of *tambu*.

27 Tolai grammar distinguishes between the inclusive and exclusive forms of the personal pronoun. 'All of us' in the inclusive sense would be 'Dat'.

28 The word 'Baining' itself appears to mean slave. Even today little is known ethnographically about the Bainings who have tucked themselves away in the fastnesses of the Baining Mountains. Small groups of Taulil and Sulka nowadays survive on the fringes of Tolai settlements. The Butum seem to have been completely eliminated. For some account of these groups see Parkinson (1907).

29 Richard Parkinson, a German national of British extraction, arrived on New Britain in 1882 to establish the first plantation on the Gazelle at Ralum. An extremely gifted man, he was later to produce what has become a classic of Oceanic ethnography, *Dreissig Jahre in der Südsee* (1907). I am indebted here to Dr Peter Sack of the Australian National University who drew my attention to a letter written by Parkinson to LeHunte (dated March 20, 1886) in which he refers to various skirmishes with the natives and concludes 'but I licked them with my Buka boys of whom I have 150'.

30 The item itself is of some interest and worth reproducing. 'Here is the latest illustration of air-mindedness in New Guinea. Thirty boys, mostly Tolais, approached Eric Stevens of Stevens Aviation with a request for a quotation for a price per head to cover the transport of 30 natives to Salamaua.' The purpose of the visit was to attend a football match (*Rabaul Times* September 18, 1936).

31 A letter to the *Rabaul Times* (February 8, 1929) signed 'Master' reads:

> I noticed on Sunday that a number of natives attending *lotu* [church services] were wearing shirts. This is the first time they have done so since the trouble started [a reference to the Rabaul strike], and it looks as though they have forgotten the matter, and are getting back into their habits of "all the same whiteman" ... There is no need to humiliate the boys, but they must not be allowed to lose sight of the fact that they are natives.'

32 New Guineans were expected to use only coinage. The coins had a hole in the centre so that they could be strung together.

33 Finney (1971) provides an index showing numbers of indigenous primary schoolteachers employed throughout the Territory and classified in terms of their district of origin. According to this index (calculated for the purpose on the basis of teachers per 100,000 head of population), the figure for East New Britain (i.e. the Tolai area) was 472, for Madang, with an equally long history of contact, forty-three, and for Chimbu and the Eastern Highlands, populous areas which were only effectively opened up after the Second World War, eight. Pursuing this matter further, it would be interesting to have a breakdown of student representation by district at the new University of Papua-New Guinea in Port Moresby. From casual statements by colleagues on the teaching staff it would appear that Tolai are considerably 'over-represented' there.

34 Between 1960 and 1968, the periods of my two visits, the Tolai population had changed from around 40,000 to around 60,000, a growth rate in excess of 5 per cent per annum. For further discussion see A.L. and T.S. Epstein (1962).

35 This is all the more interesting in that Tammur, now the Patron of the Association, had strongly attacked the workings of the Gazelle Local Government Council in his election campaign only a little earlier. At that time, however, his chief opponent was Vin ToBaining, then President of the Council, and a man of the older school who had for many years been a major public figure on the Gazelle (see Epstein *et al.* 1971:63; cf. Salisbury 1970:324-26).

36 For a popular account of this group, see Birmingham (1971). There are other Sephardi communities in the country, but these were established by more recent immigrants from Turkey and Cyprus. Although linked to Jewish 'umbrella' organizations of the kind sometimes referred to as the Community Chest, they also maintain their own separate communal institutions.

37 Even popular presentations like *Fiddler on the Roof*, with its nostalgiac evocation of what life was like *in der heim*, indicate clearly that the culture of the *shtetl* was already being threatened by forces operating within the wider society.

38 Steffens appears to have acquired a considerable knowledge of Jewish affairs through his contact with Abraham Cahan, whose novel *The Rise of David Levinsky* (1917) provides a classic account of the crisis of ethnic identity confronted by the Eastern European Jewish immigrants pouring into New York in the 1880s and 1890s.

39 Warner had earlier cut his anthropological teeth in field research among Australian Aborigines (Warner 1937). In initiating the 'Yankee City Series', his was the first substantial attempt to apply methods, techniques, and assumptions drawn from social anthropology to the study of a contemporary American urban community. The third volume in the series, on which I draw here, *The Social Systems of American Ethnic Groups* (1945) seeks to tell the history of adjustment of ethnic

groups to American life, and to consider their future within the wider society.

40 See, for example, Zborowski and Herzog (1952:131) who report on the position of the wife in the *shtetl*:

'It is the woman who manages the fiscal affairs of the family. It is proverbial that a true scholar "doesn't know one coin from another", but even in prosteh families the woman usually stores and dispenses the household cash, and to a large extent decides how it shall be used. She is the chief counselor, likely to have power of suasion and of veto in any matter outside the World of Torah.'

41 We are not told the total size of the Jewish Community, but in 1932 it must have exceeded 500, the number who attended the Yom Kippur service in the new synagogue that year.

42 Warner and Srole do not refer to the other various aspects of Jewish sacramentalism, but one suspects that many of the ritual acts prescribed for the individual, for example the wearing of the fringe (*Tzitzot*) or the daily laying of *tephillin* (phylacteries) in the case of the men, or the use of the ritual bath (*mikveh*) in the case of the women had also been abandoned.

43 For some account of the major strands — Orthodox, Conservative, and Reform — within contemporary American Judaism see Glazer (1972). Stated most briefly, Reform is furthest removed from Orthodoxy as it was conceived in the *shtetl*. As mentioned above, Reform was introduced to America by the German Jews; as the Eastern Europeans began to join Reform temples in increasing numbers, many of the central tenets of what Sklare and Greenblum (1967) call Classical Reform, for example refusal to acknowledge the Jews as other than a religious group and, linked with this, hostility to Zionism in any of its forms, themselves came to be revised. At the same time Reform services also began to edge back in the direction of the Orthodox model. Between these two, Conservative Judaism occupies a middle-of-the-road position.

44 Another interesting reflection of reversal is in regard to the change in arrangements for the holding of the main service of the week in the Wise Temple, the largest congregation in Lakeville, and classified by Sklare and Greenblum as Neo-Reform. In line with the integrationist ideology of Classical Reform, the main service of the week had originally been held on a Sunday. A clash developed within the congregation when a group of Neo-Reformers sought to shift the service to Friday evening and were eventually successful. It is plain that what was at issue between the parties was not just a matter of settling the most convenient and appealing time for worship. As Sklare and Greenblum observe (p.109), shifting to Friday night symbolized a return to the traditional Jewish Sabbath and, concomitantly, a rejection of the day of rest observed by the general community. There was also in this the implied criticism of the founding fathers of the Temple that in their desire to adapt Judaism to the American scene they had done violence to some of its fundamentals.

45 Of course, even under the conditions of the *shtetl*, where most children were likely to have been brought up in observant homes, they still had to attend Jewish schools. For a good account of such schooling based on his own childhood experience, see Deutscher (1968).

46 The one exception in this regard is the Einhorn Temple, the single bastion of Classical Reform in Lakeside. In line with the ideology of integration that it espouses, the Temple has shown no enthusiasm for the development of a social programme, for such activities would violate the principle that Jews should associate with other Jews only in a religious context.

47 Nor should one overlook here the importance of the synagogue as a political institution. One of Sklare's and Greenblum's respondents, a newcomer to Lakeville, remarked: 'Temples mean nothing to me ... All temples are a hodgepodge of internal politics.' For others this might provide an attraction. It is clear that the traditional *shul* did constitute an important area of competition for prestige and status (see, e.g. Zangwill 1895:*XI-XII*), but most sociological studies of modern communities, making use essentially of the interview and the attitude survey as the technique of enquiry, offer little in the way of an account of the political process within them. As evidence that the synagogue in the suburbs does have a political role, and for an entertaining but perceptive account of it, see the 'Rabbi' stories of Harry Kemmelman (1965, 1967).

48 Sklare and Greenblum do present a chapter on the image of 'the good Jew' in Lakeville, but it is based not on any spontaneous expression of viewpoint, but on the responses to a series of very specific questions.

49 The expression has perhaps gained a certain currency as the title of a well-known essay by Isaac Deutscher (1968), but it is also used at one point by Jacobs himself. It refers, of course, to one who has consciously abandoned all forms of religious observance, and whose formal links with Jewry are of the most tenuous kind.

50 For an excellent analysis of this aspect of the case, see Antonovsky's (1960) paper, 'Identity, Anxiety and the Jew'. Antonovsky suggests that the affair caused such a stir among American Jews because it brought to the surface expressions of a strong sense of anxiety, itself related to the lack of any sense of 'authentic' identity.

51 cf. Arian's (1968:183) comment that 'removing ideology from Israeli politics would be more than depriving the traveller of his map — it would mean divesting him of most of the landscape and much of his vehicle as well'.

52 In Cohen's case at least this inference is, I think, quite consistent with his explicit anti-psychological bias and his refusal to have any truck with unconscious motivation. Needless to say, as Erikson (1958:35) has observed of those biographers opposed to systematic psychological interpretation who yet permit themselves the most extensive psychologizing, there is always an implicit psychology behind the explicit anti-psychology.

53 Survivors of the Nazi 'death-camps' suggest an obvious parallel, but

traces of this formation are likely to be found among any group of survivors of some major disaster.

54 See, for example, Eldridge Cleaver (1968:100-101) who refers to the presence of ethnic self-hate among Black Americans which 'often takes the bizarre form of a racial death-wish, with many and elusive manifestations'. Cf. Erikson (1968:300).

55 For example, Hannerz (1974:56), discussing the question of entrepreneurship in ethnic contexts, makes the interesting point that the culture of Black Americans entails few specializations that would provide the basis on which to found a business in which outsiders would be handicapped by lack of know-how. By contrast, Italian and Jewish food habits could become the basis of small enterprises in which cultural expertise was at least as important as ethnic solidarity.

56 However, the marriage of a Tolai man to an Australian girl was received very differently, and led to a polarization of attitudes within the community (Epstein 1969:207).

57 I have examined this issue at length in a separate publication (in press). In particular I have sought to explain the unconscious roots of Tolai attachment to *tambu*, and therefore why it provides such an appropriate expression of the Tolai dilemma respecting their ethnic identity. We touch here, I believe, on some fascinating problems which have yet to receive the systematic attention they deserve.

## Chapter 2

1 Mitchell's (1953) data show that on any measure fertility on the Copperbelt is generally high, but unfortunately for present purposes he does not provide a breakdown of the figures by ethnic group.

2 Cf. Mitchell (1966) who has pointed out the need to distinguish between what he calls 'situational' change and 'processive' or historical change.

3 Pierre van den Berghe has drawn my attention to the fact that colonial administrators have sometimes been known to show a predilection towards peoples with a martial tradition, sometimes helping to foster it at the same time that they manipulated it. One thinks here, for example, of the massed military dancing of the Nguni peoples which has become a spectacle for tourists visiting Johannesburg. I find no convincing evidence that this has been the case for the Bemba. On the contrary, because the Bemba put up no effective resistance to the incoming Whites, few Europeans think of them as having been warlike people. Indeed, I frequently heard Bemba compared unfavourably in this and other regards with such people as the Zulu. Moreover, chiefs such as Chitapankwa or Mubanga Chipoya have not been established in the European mind as great historical figures as is the case, for example, with Chaka or Dingane in South Africa. Although the perception of their own history has probably been influenced by the readers produced by missionaries for use as primary school vernacular texts, it seems likely that the perpetuation of the Bemba military tradition has depended in the main on endogenous oral transmission.

4 For the reasons just mentioned, at the time I began my fieldwork in the early fifties Bemba was scarcely to be heard in Lusaka, where Nyanja was the main language spoken, and even less in Livingstone, far to the south. By the mid-fifties, however, I had the impression that the situation had already changed, and that the use of Bemba was spreading rapidly.

5 A young Bisa student referred to the matter with feeling in one of his essays. 'At this time', he wrote, 'when I am getting accustomed to speaking English or Bemba, I feel rather lonely because I cannot express my thoughts in as much as I would do in Bisa. I feel quite at home when I move in a group of my fellow Bisa and speak our pleasant language.' Bemba and Bisa are closely related languages. For others the situation may be even more difficult. Thus a Lunda father from the Mwinilunga District in the far west of the country once told me that he had to remove his children from school in Ndola and send them back home. Because of the language problem, he explained, there were always misunderstandings between them and their teachers. There may have been other considerations behind this particular decision, such as the desire to see his sons go through the rite of circumcision, but this does not affect the point at issue.

6 It is very striking to find in the records of the African Welfare Societies, the first informal groupings of younger and more educated Africans to emerge in the towns, and thence carried back to some rural communities, that the question why Africans were addressed as 'boy' was one that came up with unfailing regularity. Of some historical interest here are the minutes of the Society in Chinsali, for it was here that Kenneth Kaunda, later to become first President of Zambia, began to cut his political teeth.

7 Support for this view is to be found in Legum's brief account of some of the power struggles that were being waged at top level in the period prior to, and in the years immediately following, the winning of independence. A number of these were widely interpreted as attempts by certain groups to achieve dominance. Legum (1970:107) sums up:

'Out of this mixture of suspicion, ambition, political disagreement and personal rivalries, a new pattern of tribal alliances emerged. One of these was led by the Bemba and Tonga [of the Southern Province], the other by the Lozi and Ngoni ... These tribal alliances had no foundation in traditional history or in local interests; they were the product of a new set of conflicting interests between the modern elites in the power structure.'

It is also worth noting here that following the collapse of the Central African Federation, and the emergence of Malawi and Zambia as new nations, relations between the two countries quickly became strained, leading to demands for the return of Malawi workers in Zambia to their own country. Although a number of factors were undoubtedly at work here, it is difficult to resist the conclusion that toppling the 'Nyasas' from their occupational pedestal was an underlying consideration.

*Chapter 3*

1 It is tempting to speculate that in presenting these brief accounts of his relations with father and grandfather Reik has treated the mother (and perhaps by extension the mother's father) in much the same way as he claims Mosaic Judaism suppressed the earlier notion of a mother-goddess. Unfortunately, there is no material available to me to pursue this line of thought.

2 Having drafted this passage it occurred to me that I ought to check back in Grinstein's (1964) *The Index of Psychoanalytic Writings*. I was not wholly surprised to discover that, one item apart, the papers I refer to here are the only ones listed to the year 1953. A similar picture obtains for the period 1953-60.

3 Of some interest here is a note by Jacobson (1964:67) touching a precocious and rather aggressive little boy of one whose mutual interrelations with mother and grandmother appeared to be affectionate, but 'were already rather different in nature'.

4 But compare in this regard Erikson (1963:214 f.n.) who notes that in psychoanalytic patients met with in an American practice the overwhelming importance of the grandfather is often apparent. His further comment is also of particular interest in the present context. What these grandfathers had in common, he tells us, was that they were 'the last representatives of a more homogenous world, masterly and cruel with good conscience, disciplined and pious without loss of self-esteem'.

5 Here, as in other instances, Jewish custom, far from being static, has been subject to continuous change, development, and elaboration throughout the ages. For an account of circumcision from this point of view see Schauss (1950).

6 The London Kinship Project, focussing on the study of kinship on a middle-class sector of London, hints at a similar development there. A number of Jewish families fell within the purview of the study, and though far from conclusive, there was some evidence to suggest that Jewish families held no wider recognition of kin than their non-Jewish neighbours, though they did seem to be able to activate their own kin relations rather more effectively for ceremonies connected with their children (see Firth, Hubert, and Forge 1969:227).

7 See also in this regard Fortes (1950:277 f.n.):

'The status of grandparents explains the importance so often attached to kinship within four generations. In brief, four generations is about the maximum extension of a descent line over which all the progeny of a man or a woman can remain united either under his or her authority or through living contact with him or her ... The "grandparents" are decisive in this chain of living contact as they form the bridge between *their* grandparents and their grandchildren.'

# REFERENCES

Abraham, K. 1913. Some Remarks on the Role of the Grandparents in the Psychology of Neurosis. Reprinted in *Clinical Papers and Essays on Psychoanalysis*, Vol. 2 (1955). New York: Basic Books.

Antonovsky, A. 1960. Identity, Anxiety and the Jew'. In M.R. Stein, A.D. Vidich, and D.M. White (eds.), *Identity and Anxiety: Survival of the Person in Mass Society*. Glencoe: Free Press.

Apple, D. 1956. The Social Structure of Grandparenthood. *American Anthropologist 58:* 656-63.

Apthorpe, R. 1968. Does Tribalism really matter? *Transition 7:* 18-22.

Arian, A. 1968. *Ideological Change in Israel*. Cleveland: Case Western Reserve University Press.

Baessler, A. 1895. *Südsee-Bilder*. Berlin: Georg Reimer.

Banton, M. 1957. *West African City*. London: Oxford University Press for International African Institute.

Barth, F. 1969. *Ethnic Groups and Boundaries*. Boston: Little Brown & Co.

Berlin, I. 1959. *The Life and Opinions of Moses Hess*. Cambridge: Heffers for the Jewish Historical Society of England.

Berman, L. 1968. *Jews and Intermarriage*. New York: Thomas Yoseloff.

Birmingham, S. 1971. *The Grandees: America's Sephardi Elite*. New York: Harper & Row.

Blau, J.L. 1965. The Spiritual Life of American Jewry. In *The Characteristics of American Jews*. New York: Jewish Education Committee Press.

Blum, H. 1900. *Neu Guinea ünd der Bismarck-Archipel*. Berlin: Schönfeld.

Bowlby, J. 1961. Processes of Mourning. *International Journal of Psychoanalysis 42:* 317-38.

————— 1973: *Attachment and Loss. Vol. 2 Separation*. London: Hogarth Press.

Bürger, F. 1923. *Ünter den Kannibalen der Südsee*. Dresden: Deutsche Buchwerkstätten.

Burridge, K. 1960. *Mambu: A Melanesian Millenium*. London: Methuen.

Cahan, A. 1917. *The Rise of David Levinsky*. New York: Harper & Row.

Campbell, B. 1967. *Human Evolution: an Introduction to Man's Adaptations*. London: Heinemann.

Caplan, G. 1970. *The Elites of Barotseland 1878-1969*. London: C. Hurst.

Charsley, S.R. 1974. The Formation of Ethnic Groups. In A. Cohen (ed.), *Urban Ethnicity*. London: Tavistock Publications.

Chowning, A. 1969. Recent Acculturation between Tribes in Papua-New Guinea. *Journal of Pacific History 4*: 27-40.

Cleaver, E. 1968. *Soul on Ice*. New York: McGraw Hill.

Cohen, A. 1969. *Custom and Politics in Urban Africa*. Berkeley: University of California Press.

———— 1974a. Introduction: The Lesson of Ethnicity. In A. Cohen (ed.), *Urban Ethnicity*. London: Tavistock Publications.

———— 1974b. *Two-Dimensional Man*. Berkeley: University of California Press.

Colson, E. 1953. Clans and the Joking Relationship among the Plateau Tonga. Reprinted in *The Plateau Tonga of Northern Rhodesia* (1962). Manchester: Manchester University Press.

Dennis, N. 1955. *Cards of Identity*. London: Weidenfeld and Nicholson.

Deutscher, I. 1968. *The Non-Jewish Jew and Other Essays*. London: Oxford University Press.

Epstein, A.L. 1953. *The Administration of Justice and the Urban African*. London: HMSO.

———— 1958. *Politics in an Urban African Community*. Manchester: Manchester University Press.

———— 1959. Linguistic Innovation and Culture on the Copperbelt. *Southwestern Journal of Anthropology 15*: 235-53.

———— 1961a. The Network and Urban Social Organization. *Rhodes-Livingstone Journal 24*: 29-62. Reprinted in J.C. Mitchell (ed.), *Social Networks in Urban Situations* (1969). Manchester: Manchester University Press.

———— 1961b. New Guinea — Fast or Slow? The Tolai of the Gazelle Peninsula. *Journal of the Polynesian Society 70*: 492-96.

———— 1964. Urban Communities in Africa. In M. Gluckman (ed.), *Closed Systems and Open Minds*. Edinburgh: Oliver & Boyd.

———— 1967. Urbanization and Social Change in Africa. *Current Anthropology 8*: 275-84.

———— 1969. *Matupit: Land, Politics and Change among the Tolai of New Britain*. Berkeley: University of California Press.

———— 1971. Autonomy and Identity: Aspects of Political Development on the Gazelle Peninsula. *Anthropological Forum 2*: 427-43.

———— 1975. Military Organization and the Pre-colonial Policy of the Bemba of Zambia. *Man 10*. 201-19.

# 170 *Ethos and Identity*

Epstein, A.L. (in press). *Tambu:* the Shell-money of the Tolai.

―――― *et al.* 1971. Under the Volcano. In A.L. Epstein, R.S. Parker, and Marie Reay (eds.), *The Politics of Dependence: Papua New Guinea 1968.* Canberra: Australian National University Press.

Epstein, A.L. and T.S. 1962. A Note on Population in Two Tolai Settlements. *Journal of the Polynesian Society 71:* 70-82.

Epstein, T.S. 1968. *Capitalism, Primitive and Modern: Some Aspects of Tolai Economic Growth.* Canberra: Australian National University Press.

Erikson, E.H. 1958. *Young Man Luther.* New York: Norton.

―――― 1963. *Childhood and Society.* New York: Norton. Second edition.

―――― 1968. *Identity: Youth and Crisis.* New York: Norton.

Ferenczi, S. 1913. The Grandfather Complex. Reprinted in *Further Contributions to the Theory and Technique of Psychoanalysis* (1952). New York: Basic Books.

Finney, R. 1971. *Would-be Entrepreneurs? A Study of Motivation in New Guinea.* New Guinea Research Bulletin No. 41.

Firth, R. (ed.) 1956. *Two Studies of Kinship in London.* London: The Athlone Press.

Firth, R., Hubert, J., and Forge, A. 1969. *Families and their Relatives.* London: Routledge & Kegan Paul.

Flügel, J. 1948. *The Psychoanalytic Study of the Family.* London: Hogarth Press.

Fortes, M. 1950. Kinship and Marriage among the Ashanti. In A. Radcliffe-Brown and D. Forde (eds.), *African System of Kinship and Marriage.* London: Oxford University Press for the International African Institute.

Freud, S. 1909. Family Romances. Standard Edition Vol. 9. London: Hogarth Press.

Geertz, C. 1963. The Integrative Revolution. In C. Geertz (ed.), *Old Societies and New States.* Glencoe: Free Press.

Glazer, N. 1965. *Social Characteristics of American Jews.* New York: Jewish Education Committee Press.

―――― 1972. *American Judaism.* Chicago: University of Chicago Press. Second edition.

Glazer, N. and Moynihan, D.P. 1963. *Beyond the Melting Pot.* Cambridge: Massachusetts Institute of Technology and Harvard University Press.

―――― 1974. Why Ethnicity? *Commentary 58:* 33-9.

―――― 1975. *Ethnicity: Theory and Experience.* Cambridge: Harvard University Press.

Gluckman, H.M. 1945. The Seven Year Research Plan of the Rhodes-Livingstone Institute. *Rhodes-Livingstone Journal 4:* 1-32.

Goody, J. (ed.) 1958. *The Developmental Cycle in Domestic Groups.* Cambridge: Cambridge Univeristy Press.

Gordon, M. 1964. *Assimilation in American Life.* New York: Oxford University Press.

Grinstein, A. 1964. *The Index of Psychoanalytic Writings*. New York: International Universities Press.

Gutkind, P.C.W. 1966. African Urban Chiefs: Agents of Stability or Change in African Urban Life? *Anthropologica 8:* 249-68.

Guttmann, A. 1971. *The Jewish Writer in America*. New York: Oxford University Press.

Gyomroi, E.L. 1963. The Analysis of a Young Concentration Camp Victim. *Psycho-analytic Study of the Child 18:* 484-510.

Hannerz, U. 1974. Ethnicity and Opportunity in Urban America. In A. Cohen (ed.), *Urban Ethnicity*. London: Tavistock Publications.

Harries-Jones, P.J. 1969. Home-boy Ties and Political Organization in a Copperbelt Township. In J.C. Mitchell (ed.), *Social Networks in Urban Situations*. Manchester: Manchester University Press.

Hess, M. 1918. *Rome and Jerusalem*. New York: Bloch.

Hogbin, H.I. and Wedgwood, C. 1953. Local Groupings in Melanesia. *Oceania 23:* 241-76.

Jacobs, P. 1965. *Is Curly Jewish?* New York: Vintage Books.

Jacobson, E. 1964. *The Self and the Object World*. New York: International Universities Press.

Jones, E. 1913a. The Significance of the Grandfather for the Fate of the Individual. Reprinted in *Papers on Psycho-Analysis* (1923). London: Bailliere, Tindall and Cox. Third edition.

_____ 1913b. The Fantasy of Reversal of Generations. Reprinted in *Papers on Psycho-Analysis* (1923). London: Bailliere, Tindall and Cox. Third edition.

Katz, J. 1961. *Tradition and Crisis*. New York: Collier-Macmillan.

Kemmelman, H. 1965. *Friday the Rabbi Slept Late*. London: Hutchinson.

_____ 1967. *Saturday the Rabbi Went Hungry*. London: Hutchinson.

Kleintitschen, A. 1906. *Die Küstenbewohner der Gazelle Halbinsel*. Hiltrup.

Kramer, J.R. and Leventman, S. 1961. *Children of the Gilded Ghetto*. New Haven: Yale University Press.

Kuper, H. 1950. Kinship among the Swazi. In A. Radcliffe-Brown and D. Forde (eds.), *African Systems of Kinship and Marriage*. London: Oxford University Press for the International African Institute.

Kuper, L. 1965. *An African Bourgeoisie*. New Haven: Yale University Press.

Lawrence, P. and Meggitt, M.J. (eds.) 1965. *Gods, Ghosts and Men in Melanesia*. Melbourne: Melbourne University Press.

Leach, E.R., 1967. *A Runaway World*. London: Oxford University Press.

Legum, C. 1970. Tribal Survival in the Modern African Political System. *Journal of Asian and African Studies 5:* 102-12.

Leslie, S.C. 1971. *The Rift in Israel*. London: Routledge & Kegan Paul.

Lichtenstein, H. 1963. The Dilemma of Human Identity. *Journal of the American Psychoanalytic Association 11:* 173-223.

Lifton, R.J. 1967. *Death in Life: Survivors of Hiroshima.* New York: Random House.

———1969. *Boundaries: Psychological Man in Revolution.* New York: Random House.

Lipset, M. and Raab, E. 1970. The Non-Generation Gap. *Commentary 50*: 35-9.

Little, K. 1965. *West African Urbanization.* Cambridge: Cambridge University Press.

Litvinoff, B. 1965. *To the House of their Fathers.* New York: Praeger.

McCulloch, M. 1956. *A Social Survey of the African Population of Livingstone.* Rhodes-Livingstone Paper No. 26. Manchester: Manchester University Press.

Magubane, B. 1969. Pluralism and Conflict Situations in Africa: A New Look. *African Social Research 7*: 529-54.

Mair, L. 1963. *New Nations.* London: Weidenfeld and Nicholson.

Mannoni, O. 1956. *Prospero and Caliban: The Psychology of Colonization.* London: Methuen.

Mayer, P. 1962. Migrancy and the Study of Africans in Towns. *American Anthropologist 64*: 576-92.

Mead, M. 1970. *Culture and Commitment.* New York: Natural History Press.

———1972. *Blackberry Winter.* New York: Simon and Schuster.

Mitchell, J.C. 1953. An Estimate of Fertility among Africans on the Copperbelt of Northern Rhodesia. *Rhodes-Livingstone Journal 13*: 18-29.

———1956. *The Kalela Dance.* Rhodes-Livingstone Paper No. 27. Manchester: Manchester University Press.

———1957. Aspects of African Marriage on the Copperbelt of Northern Rhodesia. *Rhodes-Livingstone Journal 22*: 1-29.

———1960. White-Collar Workers and Supervisors in a Plural Society. *Civilizations 3*: 293-306.

———1966. Theoretical Orientations in African Urban Studies. In M. Banton (ed.), *The Social Anthropology of Complex Societies.* London: Tavistock Publications.

———1970. Tribe and Social Change in South Central Africa: A Situational Approach. *Journal of Asian and African Studies 5*: 83-101.

Mitchell, J.C. 1973. Distance, Transportation and Urban Involvement in Zambia. In A. Southall (ed.), *Urban Anthropology.* London: Oxford University Press.

———1974. Perceptions of Ethnicity and Ethnic Behaviour: An Empirical Approach. In A. Cohen (ed.), *Urban Ethnicity.* London: Tavistock Publications.

Mitchell, J.C. and Epstein, A.L. 1959. Occupational Prestige and Social Status among Urban Africans in Northern Rhodesia. *Africa 29*: 22-39.

———1962. Power and Prestige among Africans in Northern Rhodesia: An Experiment. *Southern Rhodesia Journal of Science 45*: 13-26.

Nair, K. 1969. *The Lonely Furrow: Farming in the United States, Japan and India.* Ann Arbor: University of Michigan Press.

Panoff, M. 1969. An Experiment in Inter-Tribal Contacts. *Journal of Pacific History 4*: 111-27.

Parenti, M. 1967. Ethnic Politics and the Persistence of Ethnic Identifications. *American Political Science Review 61*: 717-26.

Parker, R.S. 1971. From Dependence to Autonomy? In A.L. Epstein, R.S. Parker, and Marie Reay (eds.), *The Politics of Dependence: Papua New Guinea 1968.* Canberra: Australian National University Press.

Parkinson, R. 1907. *Dreissig Jahre in der Südsee.* Stuttgart: Strecker und Schröder.

Polansky, E.A. 1965. The Rabaul Open and West Gazelle Special Electorates. In D.G. Bettison, C.A. Hughes and P.W. Vander Veur (eds.), *The Papua-New Guinea Elections 1964.* Canberra: Australian National University Press.

Radcliffe-Brown, A. 1950. Introduction. In A. Radcliffe-Brown and D. Forde (eds.), *African Systems of Kinship and Marriage.* London: Oxford University Press for the International African Institute.

_____ 1952. *Structure and Function in Primitive Society.* London: Cohen and West.

Rappaport, E. 1958. The Grandparent Syndrome. *Psychoanalytic Quarterly 27*: 518-37.

Reay, M. 1971. Free Elections in a Guided Democracy. In A.L. Epstein, R.S. Parker, and Marie Reay (eds.), *The Politics of Dependence: Papua New Guinea 1968.* Canberra: Australian National University Press.

Reik, T. 1948. *Listening with the Third Ear.* New York: Grove Press.

_____ 1964. *Pagan Rites in Judaism.* New York: Farrar, Strauss.

Roberts, A. 1974. *A History of the Bemba.* Harlow: Longmans.

Rogow, A. (ed.) 1961. *The Jew in a Gentile World.* New York: Macmillan.

Rotberg. R. 1965. *Christian Missions and the Creation of Northern Rhodesia.* Princeton: Princeton University Press.

Roth, P. 1959. *Good-bye Columbus and Five Short Stories.* Boston: Houghton Mifflin.

Salisbury, R. 1970 *Vunamami: Economic Transformation in a Traditional Society.* Berkeley: University of California Press.

Samuel, M. 1948. *Prince of the Ghetto.* Philadelphia: Jewish Publication Society of America.

Schauss, H. 1950. *The Lifetime of a Jew.* New York: Union of American Hebrew Congregations.

Schneider, D. 1968. *American Kinship: A Cultural Account.* Englewood Cliffs, New Jersey: Prentice-Hall.

Sklare, M. and Greenblum, J. 1967. *Jewish Identity on the Suburban Frontier.* New York: Basic Books.

Southall, A. 1970. The Illusion of Tribe. *Journal of Asian and African Studies 5*: 28-50.

Stein, H.D. 1965. Jewish Social Work in the United States. In *Characteristics of American Jews*. New York: Jewish Education Committee Press.

Van den Berghe, P. 1965. Introduction. In *Africa: Social Problems of Change and Conflict*. San Francisco: Chandler.

Warner, W.L. 1937. *A Black Civilization*. New York: Harper & Row.

Warner, W. L. and Srole, L. 1945. *The Social Systems of American Ethnic Groups*. New Haven: Yale University Press.

Watson, W. 1958. *Tribal Cohesion in a Money Economy*. Manchester: Manchester University Press.

Wheelis, A. 1958. *The Quest for Identity*. New York: Norton.

Wiesel, E. 1972. *Souls on Fire*. New York: Random House.

Wilson, G. 1940. *The Economics of Detribalization*. Rhodes-Livingstone Papers Nos. 5 and 6. Manchester: Manchester University Press.

Wilson, G. and M. 1954. *The Analysis of Social Change*. Cambridge: Cambridge University Press.

Wirth, L. 1928. *The Ghetto*. Chicago: University of Chicago Press.

———— 1938. Urbanism as a Way of Life. *American Journal of Sociology 44*: 1-24.

Wolfe, B. 1965. *Marxism*. New York: Dial Press.

Wolfe, T. 1935. *Of Time and the River*. New York: Scribner.

Young, J.Z. 1971. *An Introduction to the Study of Man*. Oxford: Clarendon Press.

Zangwill, I. 1895. *Children of the Ghetto*. London: Macmillan.

Zborowski, M. and Herzog, E. 1952. *Life is with People*. New York: International Universities Press.

# NAME INDEX

# SUBJECT INDEX